MORE
GREAT
TEACHINGS OF
EDGAR CAYCE

A.R.E. MEMBERSHIP SERIES

MORE
GREAT
TEACHINGS OF
EDGAR CAYCE

by Mark Thurston, Ph.D.,
and the
Editors of the A.R.E.

ARE
PRESS

**ASSOCIATION FOR
RESEARCH AND
ENLIGHTENMENT**

A.R.E. Press • Virginia Beach • Virginia

A.R.E. Press
Sixty-Eighth & Atlantic Avenue
P.O. Box 656
Virginia Beach, VA 23451-0656

Thurston, Mark.
   More great teachings of Edgar Cayce / by Mark Thurston ;
and the editors of the A.R.E.
      p.   cm.—(A.R.E. membership series)
   ISBN 0-87604-396-1 (trade paper)
   1. Cayce, Edgar, 1877-1945.—Edgar Cayce readings. 2. Para-
psychology.   3. Occultism.   I. Association for Research and
Enlightenment. II. Title. III. Series.
BP605.A77T485   1997
133'.8'092—dc21   97-33439

The A.R.E. Membership Series

This book, *More Great Teachings of Edgar Cayce*, is another in a continuing series of books that is published by the Association for Research and Enlightenment, Inc., for individuals who are especially interested in their personal and spiritual growth and transformation.

The A.R.E. was founded in 1931 as a nonprofit organization to study, research, and disseminate information on holistic health, vocational guidance, spiritual growth, dreams, meditation, life after death, and dozens of other subjects. The A.R.E. continues its mission today, nurturing a worldwide membership with conferences, study groups, and a variety of publications—all aimed at helping seekers find paths that will lead to a more fulfilling life, mentally, physically, and spiritually. The hallmark of A.R.E.'s publications is to be helpful and hopeful.

Many of the books published by A.R.E. are available in bookstores throughout the world and all are available directly from the A.R.E.'s mail-order catalogs.

Three new books in this *A.R.E. Membership Series* are sent as gifts each year to individuals who are Sponsoring members or Life members of A.R.E. Each of the titles in this series will become available, in the year after initial publication, for purchase by individuals throughout the world who are interested in individual growth and transformation.

For more information about membership benefits of the nonprofit Association for Research and Enlightenment, Inc., please turn to the last page in this volume.

The A.R.E. Membership Series:

Edgar Cayce's Approach to Rejuvenation of the Body
The Great Teachings of Edgar Cayce
Edgar Cayce's ESP
Symbols: Guiding Lights Along the Journey of Life
The Golden Thread of Oneness
More Great Teachings of Edgar Cayce

Contents

Introduction

Whether derived from books, movies, or other creative endeavors, sequels are often criticized for not living up to the quality of the first installment. But the breadth of topics and the depth of wisdom of the Cayce material made it relatively simple for me to produce a second volume of highlights from this man's groundbreaking work. Just as I did a year and a half earlier with *The Great Teachings of Edgar Cayce*, I have attempted in the present volume to highlight the core of Edgar Cayce's work.

If any of us were so fortunate as to receive a reading of our own from Cayce, the personal help received would probably make us decide that that very reading was one of the "great" ones. But in selecting just sixteen readings for this book, I've looked for instances in which the wisdom and insight demonstrated by Cayce have a universal appeal. The ones I've chosen fit into four categories, creating the four sections of the book. Each category illustrates Edgar Cayce in a particular role, as a special kind of teacher or wisdom figure. For each selected reading I've added an interpretive commentary which I hope will be useful in underlining key principles.

The first role featured in this book is Edgar Cayce the

social visionary. We don't really understand the man and his work unless we see how committed he was to healing and reconciliation at many levels: community, national, and international. He saw a world in which the influences of evil and selfishness are a very real threat. But his view was fundamentally a hopeful one, and it always affirmed the potential for greatness within each individual and the human family collectively.

Second is Edgar Cayce the guide along our journey as souls. He always saw life as a challenging pilgrimage in which we are called to be cocreators with God. As we see ourselves as souls in the making, each with special talents and purposes, life becomes an inspiring adventure.

Third is Edgar Cayce the prophet of changing times. To many people this is Cayce's most familiar role. And although his readings about changing times make up only a tiny fraction of the 14,306 readings in the archival records, those discourses are among his most important and universally significant.

Fourth is Edgar Cayce the teacher of balanced living. For many students of this material, nothing has been more important to them than Cayce's practical suggestions for how to live in a material world while simultaneously affirming the reality of a spiritual world. It can be a delicate balancing act "to be in the world but not of it," and the Cayce material contains some of the finest and most useful suggestions for attuned daily living.

While it would be presumptuous ever to claim that one had completely caught the essence of Cayce's teachings, these four roles and the readings that illustrate them surely reveal the greatness of this man's work and the philosophy he taught. These readings—along with the ones in the earlier volume—are a wonderful introduction for anyone new to this material, and at the same time they are a powerful way to reconnect with the heart of this man's work for even the most experienced student.

Chapter 1

THE PROBLEM OF GOOD AND EVIL

READING 262-52

What are we to make of violence, greed, and selfish ambition—some of the faces of so-called evil? How does a person who is trying to view the world from a spiritual perspective understand the blatant use of power and influence to harm others?

Some of the most insightful comments from the Cayce readings on the problem are found in this reading for the original "A Search for God" group. It was delivered in the midst of their study of the lesson "Opportunity." Nothing could be more fitting, since the essential opportunity we will face in materiality is choosing what we will serve: life-promoting values or destructive, selfish ones. As we find near the end of this reading: " . . . will is given to man . . . for the choice."

As we see from the suggestion that was given to Cayce, the primary intent of the reading was to obtain a systematic set of principles about *oneness*—fundamental truths that could be presented to students. No doubt several members of the group remembered that four years earlier an accomplished scholar of the Cayce readings, Morton Blumenthal, had a similar desire to create a curriculum of spiritual teachings for serious students. The advice to him had been, "The first lesson for *six months* should be *One*—One—*One;* Oneness of God, oneness of man's relation, oneness of force, oneness of time, oneness of purpose, *oneness* in every effort—oneness—oneness!" (900-429)

Although what makes reading 262-52 especially noteworthy is the question-and-answer exchange concerning evil, an invaluable context is set in the main body of the reading. In fact, it's hard to appreciate Cayce's angle on good and evil unless we first grasp his story of creation and the law of oneness.

God is the first cause, the one source. And in the great, creative act that gave birth to the universe, God "moved." Polar opposites were the result: attraction and repulsion, positive and negative. A realm of experience came into being that offers the choice between options. That dynamic tension was the key to what lay ahead.

Where does the human soul fit into this story? Each of us was created with a goal in mind—a possibility for what we could become. With the gift of free will, each of us was a being of choice—capable of following the plan for our development *or* of rebelling. In the plan of spiritual evolution the infinite spirit penetrates matter—that is, the universal spirit comes to know itself in individualized form. It's man's opportunity to "be aware of that first cause moving within his realm of consciousness."

So how has humanity gone wrong? How has error or evil entered in? We are tempted by two fundamental forms of evil that are alluded to by Cayce and more explicitly described by other spiritual philosophers such as Martin Buber and Rudolf Steiner. Both forms of evil are a type of rebellion, as Cayce puts it. Both mean going against the evolutionary impulse that would bring the infinite spirit consciously into the finite, material world.

One sort of evil influences men and women to believe that there is no spiritual reality. It denies the oneness of

God—or even the presence of a higher realm. It leads us to resist that "inter-penetrating" spirit and to focus exclusively on physical reality. The result can be blind materialism, the fear of death, and coldhearted, self-interested logic.

The other sort of evil is harder to recognize. It claims more for ourselves than we're entitled to. In spite of our self-illusions, we really aren't the *source* of the one, creative energy; we are merely able to direct it and *reflect* it. Cayce's analogy asks us to think about a mirror, something that doesn't emit its own light but simply reflects light and redirects its path. This type of evil admits to the reality of the spiritual realm but leads a man or woman to make a critical misstep—the claim to be the source rather than a reflector, to say "I am God" rather than "I serve the one God who lives in me."

Is there a particular *being* that leads us astray, a personal devil? This reading speaks of one. But that is *not* equivalent to saying that evil is a person, any more than a "personal God" means that God is literally a super-person. Instead, Cayce is reminding us that *each person has his or her own relationship* to the influence of evil—that spirit of rebellion that leads us away from the true purpose of life.

This is not the idle stuff of philosophers and theologians. It hits right at the heart of our modern culture and the mess we've gotten ourselves into. We're groping for the values that will revitalize and heal our society. The starting point should be—even as it was in this reading—the underlying oneness of God. Next comes seeing that some choices really are life promoting and others aren't. In other words, we've got to face the fact courageously that the influence of evil is very real. It's not a separate power apart from God; instead it's a rebellious way of using that one source. Ultimately, confronting the problem of good and evil isn't so much a matter of unraveling a philosophical knot. Rather, it's something much more simple and direct, something that virtually every Cayce reading tries to bring people back to: the willingness to take responsibility for our choices.

THE READING

This psychic reading, 262-52, was given by Edgar Cayce on August 25, 1933. The conductor was Gertrude Cayce.

[1]GC: You will give at this time a discourse which will sum up and correlate the data already given through this channel on the fundamental truths regarding the Oneness of all Force, and will furnish us with some basic, logical, systematically arranged statements which can be given out as fundamental truths to students of this work. You will answer the questions on this subject which will be asked.

[2]EC: Yes. In giving that which may be given out as basic truth, and correlating the statements that have been made from time to time, it would have been better to have gathered from that given the basis for expansion through these channels.

[3]Yet, we may give that which may be the basis or the foundation of truth that may be gathered here and there.

[4]As to the correlation and the setting out of paragraphs, at least you should do something!

[5]The basis, then: "Know, O Israel, (Know, O People) the Lord Thy God is One!"

[6]From this premise we would reason, that: In the manifestation of all power, force, motion, vibration, that which impels, that which detracts, is in its essence of one force, one source, in its elemental form. As to what has been done or accomplished by or through the activity of entities that have been delegated powers in activity is another story.

[7]As to the one source or one force, then, are the questions presented in the present.

[8]God, the first cause, the first principle, the first movement, *is!* That's the beginning! That is, that was, that ever shall be!

[9]The following of those sources, forces, activities that are in accord with the Creative Force or first cause—its laws, then—is to be one with the source, or equal with yet separate from that first cause.

[10]When, then, may man—as an element, an entity, a separate being manifested in material life and form—be aware or conscious of the moving of that first cause within his own environ?

[11]Or, taking man in his present position or consciousness, how or when may he be aware of that first cause moving within his realm of consciousness?

[12]In the beginning there was the force of attraction and the force that repelled. Hence, in man's consciousness he becomes aware of what is known as the atomic or cellular form of movement about which there becomes nebulous activity. And this is the lowest form (as man would designate) that's in active forces in his experience. Yet this very movement that separates the forces in atomic influence is the first cause, or the manifestation of that called God in the material plane!

[13]Then, as it gathers of positive-negative forces in their activity, whether it be of one element or realm or another, it becomes magnified in its force or sources through the universe.

[14]Hence we find worlds, suns, stars, nebulae, and whole solar systems *moving* from a first cause.

[15]When this first cause comes into man's experience in the present realm he becomes confused, in that he appears to have an influence upon this force or power in directing same. Certainly! Much, though, in the manner as the reflection of light in a mirror. For, it is only re-

flected force that man may have upon those forces that show themselves in the activities, in whatever realm into which man may be delving in the moment—whether of the nebulae, the gaseous, or the elements that have gathered together in their activity throughout that man has chosen to call time or space. And becomes, in its very movement, of that of which the first cause takes thought *in* a finite existence or consciousness.

[16]Hence, as man applies himself—or uses that of which he becomes conscious in the realm of activity, and gives or places the credit (as would be called) in man's consciousness in the correct sphere or realm he becomes conscious of that union of force with the infinite with the finite force.

[17]Hence, in the fruits of that—as is given oft, as the fruits of the spirit—does man become aware of the infinite penetrating, or inter-penetrating the activities of all forces of matter, or that which is a manifestation of the realm of the infinite into the finite—and the finite becomes conscious of same.

[18]As to the application of these as truths, then:

[19]It may be said that, as the man makes in self—through the ability given for man in his activity in a material plane—the will one with the laws of creative influence, we begin with:

[20]"Like begets like—As he sows, so shall he reap—As the man thinketh in the heart, so is he."

[21]These are all but trite sayings to most of us, even the thinking man; but should the mind of an individual (the finite mind) turn within his own being for the law pertaining to these trite sayings, until the understanding arises, then there is the consciousness in the finite of the infinite moving upon and in the inner self.

[22]So does life in all its force begin in the earth. The moving of the infinite upon the negative force of the finite in the material, or to become a manifested force.

²³Ready for questions.

²⁴(Q) Explain how so-called good and evil forces are one.

(A) This has just been explained. When there is delegated power to a body that has separated itself from the spirit (or coming from the unseen into the seen, or from the unconscious into the physical consciousness, or from God's other door—or opening from the infinite to the finite), then the activity is life; with the will of the source of that which has come into being. As to what it does with or about its associations of itself to the source of its activity, as to how far it may go afield, depends upon how high it has attained in its ability to throw off both negative and positive forces.

Hence we say, "The higher he flies the harder the fall." It's true!

Then, that which has been separated into the influence to become a body, whether celestial, terrestrial, or plain clay manifested into activity as man, becomes good or bad. The results to the body so acting are dependent and independent [interdependent?] (inter-between, see) upon what he does with the knowledge of—or that source of—activity.

²⁵(Q) In relation to the Oneness of all force, explain the popular concept of the Devil, seemingly substantiated in the Bible by many passages of scripture.

(A) In the beginning, celestial beings. We have first the Son, then the other sons or celestial beings that are given their force and power.

Hence that force which rebelled in the unseen forces (or in spirit) that came into activity, was that influence which has been called Satan, the Devil, the Serpent; they are One. That of *rebellion!*

Hence, when man in any activity rebels against the influences of good he harkens to the influence of evil rather than the influence of good.

Hence, will is given to man as he comes into this manifested form that we see in material forces, for the choice. As given, "There is set before thee (man) good and evil."

Evil is rebellion. Good is the Son of Life, of Light, of Truth; and the Son of Light, of Life, of Truth, came into physical being to demonstrate and show and lead the way for man's ascent to the power of good over evil in a material world.

As there is, then, a personal savior, there is the personal devil.

[26]We are through.

Chapter 2

EDGAR CAYCE'S DEFINITION OF GREATNESS

READING 518-2

The modern world pushes us to believe that greatness lies in notoriety. If something is well known, well advertised, or a part of everyday conversation, then it must be something special. Nothing could be further from Edgar Cayce's definition of greatness and the life well lived. In his philosophy, *service done with humility* characterizes worthwhile living. As stated in paragraph 6: "Not to be *seen* of men, but that the love may be manifested . . . "

This theme weaves through a mental-spiritual reading for Ms. [518], a twenty-five year old who was searching for a deeper sense of purpose. Just eighteen months earlier, Cayce had given her a life reading. It was full of past-life scenarios and advice that largely confused her. She had written back, "I think my life reading is wonderful, but I don't understand it." Both Edgar and Hugh Lynn Cayce offered interpretive ideas. Her second reading was designed to address further questions, because she was still unclear about how to pursue her soul development.

The opening discourse of this reading is one of Cayce's finest statements of the universal principles governing soul growth. It has a special emphasis on joyful service undertaken with patient humility. To some scholars of the Cayce material, paragraph 3 is his most succinct and incisive description of the universal purpose for human life. It's a journey to become more conscious and to be cleansed so that we can become companions with our Creator.

Ms. [518] must have been inspired by these words. No doubt she also wondered how these lofty ideas fit the more mundane problems she faced. In her first reading she said she was perplexed about her choice of a vocation. And, in fact, this reading goes on to address her individual needs for understanding, while at the same time returning time and again to universal principles from which we can all benefit.

Rather than focus on an occupation, Cayce focuses on a *way of living* that could lead to soul development and happiness, no matter what career path she follows. Instead of counsel about a specific sort of job that would promote soul growth, we find Cayce's sense of an optimal way in life—something that may remind us of another wisdom tradition, the Tao. In Cayce's version of such a "way," the key is joyful service which puts aside self-centered desires.

What can block humble service and the soul growth it would bring? In traditional theological language, it's sin—hardly a word that many of us want to address seriously because of all the baggage it brings along. But Cayce's philosophy and his psychological advice to Ms. [518] address the possibility head-on. Selfishness, grudges, and wrath are soul patterns that maintain a separation between God and Ms. [518]'s spiritual identity (that is, the "individuality" or the "I AM" as it's called in paragraph 6). In paragraph 7, another kind of obstacle—or pattern of sin or separation—is warned against: willfulness that focuses on private fulfillment. We all have to guard against that, as much today as sixty years ago. We get off the mark when we "intentionally turn our backs" on spiritual opportunities, particularly in social relations. With that clear warning, this reading returns to hopeful themes. In fact, paragraphs 8, 9, and 16 are the spiritual heart of this reading. Great joy is available to anyone who makes an effort to lift the consciousness of someone else.

In paragraph 9 a two-phase purpose of living is described. The first component is knowledge-based: "That ye might know the Lord and *His* goodness." And then a service component can come into play as we "become as a messenger in thy service and thy activity before thy fellow man." Note that service (no matter how patient or humble) doesn't stand alone, out of context. It grows out of understanding and knowledge. For example, see if you can remember a time in your own life when you may have unintentionally created more harm than good out of your efforts to serve. If that first component—knowledge or understanding—was missing, then the deeds intended as service may not have produced the helpful results hoped for.

Cayce's answer to Ms. [518]'s first question (i.e., paragraph 16) is an eloquent summary of just the sort of humble service to which she is called—to which we *all* are called. And as our souls mature, that way of being no longer requires an effort. It becomes the natural way. It "fits us like a glove."

And when things aren't going well, in spite of service born of high ideals and good intentions, there is one final principle that we need to keep in mind. Cayce saves it for the conclusion of paragraph 16. To bring anything into manifestation, we reach a point in the process where it's outside of our conscious control. To recognize the truth in this principle, think about the important events and changes in your life, especially the ones where you've had to work hard to bring about something new. Wasn't there a stage in that process where you had to "Leave the *results* . . . with the Lord"? It's that capacity to surrender and trust which insures that our humble service really will bear fruit.

THE READING

This psychic reading, 518-2, was given by Edgar Cayce on August 13, 1935. The conductor was Gertrude Cayce.

(GC: Mental and spiritual reading, giving the original purpose of entrance into this solar realm of experience, trace the mental and spiritual development from the beginning through the various stages of experience, and give such guidance as the entity needs in awakening her psychic soul faculties and in using same for the highest spiritual development in this life. You will answer the questions she has submitted, as I ask them.)

[1]EC: Yes, we have the entity and those experiences in the mental and soul forces of same, as may be applicable in the experience in the present; that may make that necessary for the entity's development and to bring the influences that are necessary for the understanding.

[2]In tracing the experiences of the entity, and in giving purposes, aims, desires, let these be set as the law; or as the ideal manner of approach to any of such conditions:

[3]First, the entering of *every* soul is that it, the soul, may become more and more aware or conscious of the Divine within, that the soul-body may be purged that it may be a fit companion for the *glory* of the Creative Forces in its activity.

[4]The activity for this entity, then, is the same; that it may have the opportunity. For it has been given that the *Lord* hath not willed that any soul should perish. But with every temptation He hath prepared a way; so that if he or she as the erring one will turn to Him for that aid, it may find same.

[5]Then again, in the appearances, do not look or seek for the phenomenon of the experience without the purpose, the aim. *Use* same as a criterion, as what to do and what not to do. Not that it, the simple experience, has made or set *anything* permanent! For there is the constant change evidenced before us; until the soul has been washed clean through that the soul in its body, in its temple, has *experienced* by the manner in which it has acted, has spoken, has thought, has desired in its relationships to its fellow man!

[6]Not in selfishness, not in grudge, not in wrath; not in *any* of those things that make for the separation of the I AM from the Creative Forces, or Energy, or God. But the simpleness, the gentleness, the humbleness, the faithfulness, the long-suffering, *patience!* These be the attributes and those things which the soul takes cognizance of in its walks and activities before men. Not to be *seen* of men, but that the love may be manifested as the Father has shown through the Son and in the earth day by day. Thus He keeps the bounty, thus He keeps the conditions such that the individual soul may—if it will but meet or look within—find indeed *His* Presence abiding ever.

[7]The soul, the individual that purposely, intentionally, turns the back upon these things, choosing the satisfying of the own self's desire, then has turned the back upon the living God.

[8]Not that there is not to be joy, pleasure, and those things that maketh not afraid in the experience of every soul. But the joy in service, the joy in labor for the fellow man, the joy in giving of self that those through thy feeble efforts may have put before them, may become aware in their consciousness, that *thou* hast been with, that *thou* hast taken into thine own bosom the law of the Lord; and that ye walk daily with Him.

[9]What, ye say then, was the purpose for which ye en-

tered in at this particular experience? That ye might know the Lord and *His* goodness the more in thine inner self, that ye through this knowledge might become as a messenger in thy service and thy activity before thy fellow man; as one pointing the way, as one bringing— through the feeble efforts and endeavors, through the faltering steps at times, yet *trying,* attempting to do— what the conscience in the Lord hath prompted and does *prompt* thee to do.

[10]As to thy music, in this thy hands may bring the consciousness of the harmonies that are created by the vibrations in the activities of each soul; that each other soul may, too, take hope; may, too, be *just kind,* just gentle, just patient, just humble.

[11]Not that the way of the Lord is as the sounding of the trumpet, nor as the tinkling of cymbals that His might be proclaimed; but in the still small voice, in the hours of darkness that which lightens the heart to gladness, that which brings relief to the sufferer, that which makes for patience with the wayward, that which enables those that are *hungry*—in body, in mind—to be fed upon the bread of life; that they may drink deep of the water of life, through thy efforts.

[12]These are the purposes, these are the experiences that bring in the heart and in the soul the answering of that cry, "Why—*why*—have I come into this experience?"

[13]Be ye patient; be ye quiet and *see* the glory of the Lord in that thou may do in thine efforts day by day.

[14]*Do* that thou *knowest* to do, *today!* Then leave the results, leave the rewards, leave the effects into the hands of thy God. For *He* knoweth thy heart, and He hath called—if ye will harken.

[15]Ready for questions.

[16](Q) How may I attune myself that I may be one with the Creative Forces with Christ that I may find this true relationship?

(A) Just as indicated. Let thy patience, thy tolerance, thy activity be of such a positive nature that it *fits* thee—as a glove—to be patient with thy fellow man, to minister to those that are sick, to those that are afflicted, to sit with those that are shut-in, to read with those that are losing their perception, to reason with those that are wary of the turmoils; showing brotherly love, patience, persistence in the Lord, and the love that overcometh all things.

These be the things one must do. And do find patience with self. It has been said, "Have we not piped all the day long and no one has answered?" Seekest thou, as was given from this illustration, for the gratifying of thy self? or seekest thou to be a channel of blessing to thy fellow man? They may not have answered as *thou* hast seen. They may have even shown contempt, as sneering, for thy patience and thy trouble. But *somewhere* the sun still shines; *somewhere* the day is done; for those that have grown weary, for those that have given up. The Lord abhorreth the quitter. And those temptations that come in such cases are the viewing of thine own self. Ye have hurt thyself and ye have again crucified thy Lord, when ye become impatient or speak harshly because someone has jeered or because someone has sneered or because someone has laughed at thy efforts!

Leave the *results,* leave the giving of the crown, leave the glory, with the Lord! *He* will repay! Thou sayest in thine own heart that thou believest. Then merely, simply, *act* that way! In speech, in thought, in deed.

[17](Q) What are some of my difficulties that I have to meet in the present, and how should I overcome them?

(A) These ye find day by day. They have been pointed out, and the way to meet them. *Bless* ye the Lord!

[18](Q) Am I choosing that which is best for my soul development?

(A) That must ever be answered from within. How

readest thou? Read that which has just been given thee, as to how ye shall conduct yourself toward thy fellow man. This will show thee thy shortcomings; this will show thee thy graciousness. And let thy prayer be, *"Mercy, Lord! Have mercy, Thou, upon my weakness, and give me strength in Thee!"*

[19](Q) What must I do and how to make this experience be for my soul development?

(A) It has just been given.

Bear in thy activities the fruits of the spirit that maketh for *constructive* creative force in the experience of the body.

[20](Q) What should I do in order to live the lovely life in this earth plane?

(A) One and the same as that given.

[21](Q) What are those abilities or talents that lie innate, and how can they be aroused?

(A) By the application of that thou knowest to do; and those that have been intimated ye will experience as ye apply. *Seek,* and ye shall find; *knock* and it shall be opened unto you. That thou needest to do.

[22](Q) What phase of music should I study in order to derive the most benefit?

(A) That more of the nature which to thine own inner self creates *harmonious* vibrations in the experiences of self and those about thee. That partaking of the rimes [rhymes?], the lullabies, the pastoral scenes which make for such harmonious forces, bring quiet, cheer, hope, and casting out fear.

[23](Q) What studies should I take up this fall in order to become more efficient in my life's work?

(A) Do those things that are shown thee to do, that make the preparation in the material affairs for the application of self in its relation to the work it has chosen.

[24](Q) Can you tell me if Zephus, whose companion I was in the Egyptian period and with whom I gained so

much, is now in the earth plane?

(A) We haven't Zephus.

[25](Q) Have I met him? or will I know him when I see him?

(A) We haven't Zephus.

[26](Q) Is it the destiny of souls that were united in the beginning to be reunited? or can they choose otherwise?

(A) Choose otherwise.

[27](Q) Were they united for a certain purpose; is that how they are drawn together?

(A) United; for a purpose.

[28]We are through for the present.

Chapter 3

THE POWER OF HUMAN THOUGHT AND EMOTION

READING 5757-1

Sometimes the most wonderful treasures can be found in unexpected places. Who would have thought, in scanning the hundreds of topics addressed in the Edgar Cayce readings, that one of the most meaningful statements about the human condition would be found in the rather arcane subject of sun spots? And yet in this reading, 5757-1, Cayce offered not an abstract discourse on astrophysics, but a lucid, compelling analysis of how human consciousness and the material world are interconnected.

We might say that this reading demonstrates the Cayce source at its best—a blend of metaphysical teacher and moral leader. This combination characterizes spiritual authority at its finest. The first aspect presents a picture of "how things are." Cayce the metaphysician could clairvoyantly perceive and then articulate how life works. He reported on the universal laws that operate, often invisibly, to shape our experiences. He let us in on the secrets of time, space, energy, and life itself.

However, to see the Cayce readings merely as metaphysical revelation misses the point. Their power and significance come equally from the ideals and vision they convey about human relations—their moral quality. This element of a Cayce reading can sometimes make us uncomfortable. But to skip over that part, dismissing it as Cayce's Bible-belt Christian personality slipping through, is to strip this material of its deepest relevance to today's world. It is, in fact, the moral component of his readings that gave them a life-changing quality for the thousands of people who received them.

We may not like the word "moral" (it has the unfortunate connotation of being forced to conform to someone else's standards of right and wrong), but any authentic spiritual tradition invariably includes the elements of right action and responsibility in relation to others. Cayce's repeated emphasis to love and serve ("We are our brother's keeper," and "No one gets to heaven except by leaning on the arm of someone he has helped") is an inescapable part of his work. It is reminiscent of the statement by Rudolf Steiner, a European contemporary of Cayce's, that for every one step we take in pursuit of higher knowledge, we should take three steps in the realm of character development and moral living.

It is exactly this sense of direction, purpose, and ideal that makes this information more than just another set of theories that tries to make sense of an awesome, seemingly arbitrary universe. In fact, this particular reading is based on the premise—a metaphysical one—that sun spots are not arbitrary eruptions on the surface of a huge solar furnace millions of miles away. They are not merely unfortunate occurrences that disrupt radio communications. Of course, something purely physical *is* taking place, but with his expanded perspective of how the universe runs, Cayce suggested that these events have nonmaterial causes, too. He linked sun spots to human attitudes, emotions, and will.

When we first study this reading, we're probably struck with Cayce's theory of just how potent our thoughts and feelings can be. He goes beyond astronomy and suggests that astrology, too, has something valuable to say. But then he leapfrogs over astrology (as it is commonly understood to teach that the planets and the stars influence us) and arrives at the startling conclusion that we affect the planets and the stars, most noticeably our own sun.

Even for someone familiar with the notion that "mind is the builder," this deduction may be hard to swallow. Certainly attitudes and emotions may create our physical bodies: Modern mind/body medical research is proving it. And there is even strong evidence that we help shape our material life situation by our expectations and intentions. But in this reading we're invited to think on much bigger terms: a collective psychokinesis by humanity—a psychic effect that spans millions of miles.

Neither of the two keys to this reading, however, is so much about the extraordinary powers of the mind. Instead, one central element concerns how we have misused free will. That abuse takes the form of defiance—something that God permits humans alone. It is our defiance of divine purposes that ultimately produces sun spots. It is rebellion against God's plan that creates a disruptive condition on the sun. (The reading insightfully explains solar interruptions of our broadcast communications as a kind of modern-day garble, like the tower of Babel.)

The second key to an interpretation of this reading is the social ideal to which it calls us. To help identify that moral direction, three forms of defiance are identified: hate, injustice, and lying—three ways that we misuse the will in relation to others. They are the all-too-frequent ways that we defy God's intentions for us; and as we bring them into focus, the moral dimension of this reading begins to emerge. It's a message that becomes extremely direct in the final paragraphs. Simply put: We can expect disturbances from nature (sun spots and earthquakes among them) until human beings start using their wills to choose love, justice, and truth. It is our way of "being-with-each-other" that occupies the ultimate focal point of this reading.

These honorable qualities have been taught and encouraged for centuries, so we might well ask, "Why do we need the Edgar Cayce readings to say it again?" Perhaps the answer is found in the point with which this commentary began: Cayce offered metaphysics in combination with moral imperatives. Theoretical statements about the structures, dynamics, and the laws of the universe are valuable because they equip us to be of greater help to others ("The more ye become aware of thy relationships to the universe . . . the greater thy ability to help"). But the more we know, the more we are responsible for personally ending the defiance and starting to love, to be just, and to be truthful (" . . . but *still* greater thy *responsibility* to thy fellow men").

The closing of this reading is likely to make us uncomfortable. We don't want to admit that we treat other people as if they were "dross and trash." We may squirm when Cayce asks us to imagine how the Christ feels when we defy daily the divine intentions for us. In fact, we may have abandoned traditional religion simply because we wanted to get away from moral exhortations that make us feel like we've missed the mark. We may have gotten involved in metaphysical, "New Age" teachings largely because we wanted to start feeling good about ourselves and our lives. No doubt that the Cayce readings do want us to feel good about ourselves and to enjoy discovering the mysteries of the universe. The secret, however, lies in our willingness to follow a dual pathway—a double-helix, intertwining course that weaves the excitement of metaphysical understanding with the moral responsibilities of human community.

THE READING

This psychic reading, 5757-1, was given by Edgar Cayce on June 21, 1940, at the Ninth Annual A.R.E. Congress. The conductor was Gertrude Cayce.

[1]GC: You will give at this time a discourse on what are known as sun spots, explaining the cause of these phenomena and their effect on the earth and its inhabitants.

[2]EC: In giving that as we find would be as helpful information in the experience of individuals gathered here, many conditions and phases of man's experience in the earth are to be considered.

[3]When the heavens and the earth came into being, this meant the universe as the inhabitants of the earth know same; yet there are many suns in the universe—those even about which our sun, our earth, revolve; and all are moving toward some place—yet space and time appear to be incomplete.

[4]Then time and space are but one. Yet the sun, that is the center of this particular solar system, is the center; and, as has been indicated and known of old, it is that about which the earth and its companion planets circulate, or evolve [revolve?].

[5]The beginnings of the understanding of these, and their influences upon the lives of individuals, were either thought out, evolved or interpreted by those of old, without the means of observing same as considered today necessary in order to understand.

[6]Astronomy is considered a science and astrology as foolishness. Who is correct? One holds that because of the position of the earth, the sun, the planets, they are balanced one with another in some manner, some form; yet that they have nothing to do with man's life or the expanse of life, or the emotions of the physical being in the earth.

[7]Then, why and how do the effects of the sun *so* influence other life in the earth and not affect *man's* life, man's emotions?

[8]As the sun has been set as the ruler of this solar system, does it not appear to be reasonable that it *has* an effect upon the inhabitants of the earth, as well as upon plant and mineral life in the earth?

[9]Then if not, why, how did the ancients worship the sun *as* the representative of a continuous benevolent and beneficent influence upon the life of the individual?

[10]Thus as we find given, the sun and the moon and the stars were made also—this being the attempt of the writer to convey to the individual the realization that there *is* an influence in their activity! For, remember, they—the sun, the moon, the planets—have their marching orders from the Divine, and they move in same.

[11]Man alone is given that birthright of free will. He alone may defy his God!

[12]How many of you have questioned that in thine own heart, and know that thy disobedience in the earth reflects unto the heavenly hosts and thus influences that activity of God's command! For *you*—as souls and sons and daughters of God—*defy* the living God!

[13]As the sun is made to shed light and heat upon God's children in the earth, it is then of that composition of which man is made, or of that termed the earth; yet, as ye have seen and know, there is solid matter, there is liquid, there is vapor. All are one in their various stages of consciousness or of activity for what? Man—*Godly man!* Yet when these become as in defiance to that light which was commanded to march, to show forth the Lord's glory, His beauty, His mercy, His hope—yea, His patience—do ye wonder then that there become reflected upon even the face of the sun those turmoils and strifes that have been and that are the sin of man?

[14]Whence comest this?

[15]All that was made was made to show to the sons, the souls, that God *is* mindful of His children.

[16]How do they affect man? How does a cross word affect thee? How does anger, jealousy, hate, animosity, affect thee *as* a son of God? If thou art the father of same, oft ye cherish same. If thou art the recipient of same from others, thy brethren, how does it affect thee? Much as that confusion which is caused upon the earth by that which appears as a sun spot. The disruption of communications of all natures between men is what? Remember the story, the allegory if ye choose to call it such, of the tower of Babel.

[17]Yea, ye say ye trust God, and yet want to show Him how to do it!

[18]These become, then, as the influences that would show man as to his littleness in even entertaining hate, injustice, or that which would make a lie.

[19]Be honest with thyself, as ye would ask even the ruler of thine earth—the sun—to harken to the voice of that which created it and to give its light *irrespective* of how ye act! For, as given, the sun shineth upon the just and the unjust alike, yet it is oft reflected in what happens to thee in thy journey through same.

[20]The more ye become aware of thy relationships to the universe and those influences that control same, the greater thy ability to help, to aid—the greater thy ability to rely upon the God-force within; but *still* greater thy *responsibility* to thy fellow men. For, as ye do it unto the least, ye do it unto thy Maker—even as to the sun which reflects those turmoils that arise with thee; even as the earthquake, even as wars and hates, even as the influences in thy life day by day.

[21]Then, what are the sun spots? A natural consequence of that turmoil which the sons of God in the earth reflect upon same.

²²Thus they oft bring confusion to those who become aware of same.

²³Let not your hearts be troubled; ye believe in God. Then just act like it—to others.

²⁴He has given thee a mind, a body; an earth, and land in which to dwell. He has set the sun, the moon, the planets, the stars about thee to remind thee, even as the psalmist gave, "Day unto day uttereth speech, night unto night sheweth knowledge."

²⁵These ye know, these ye have comprehended; but do ye take thought of same?

²⁶*Know* that thy mind—thy *mind*—is the builder! As what does thy soul appear? A spot, a blot upon the sun? or as that which giveth light unto those who sit in darkness, to those who cry aloud for hope?

²⁷Hast thou created hope in thy association with thy fellow men?

²⁸Ye fear and cringe when ye find that the spots upon thy sun cause confusion of any nature.

²⁹How *must* thy Savior feel, look, appear, when ye deny Him day by day; when ye treat thy fellow man as though he were as dross and trash before thee?

³⁰We are through.

Chapter 4

THE SPIRIT OF THE NATIONS

READING 3976-29

The daily news of international trends and politics is often astounding. In recent years, each passing month has provided some new development or yet another surprise: In China, flickerings of free speech are seen before they are cruelly repressed; in Poland, free elections reject the solitary power of the Communist Party; in the Soviet Union, dramatic shifts happen in governmental policy; and in Western Europe, the first steps are taken toward unification. Was there anything in the Cayce readings to predict these and other sweeping changes?

Cayce's "World Affairs" readings contain some of his most significant comments on international conditions, including prophecies and clairvoyant perspectives on the nations. Reading 3976-29, provided to the annual gathering of leaders of the Association, the 1944 Congress meeting, came just as the tide in Europe began to turn in favor of the Allies during World War II. The suggestion for the reading asked for information about the group vibrations of specific nations—that is, the spirit of that country and its people.

Compared to the familiar national stereotypes—the English reserve, the French love of life, the Japanese work ethic—Cayce's descriptions seem to cut deeper. His perspective portrays a group consciousness for individual nations, one that includes both a karmic fault and a collective aspiration. As we study the ideas in this reading, it's important to avoid becoming judgmental about the faults of various nations. We may well have had incarnations in those countries and may have ourselves contributed to those patterns of weakness.

The reading begins with a cosmic picture. Before the nations came into being, souls faced a spiritual choice. On the one hand was God's intention for us—companionship with the Creator—but on the other hand was the impulse to defy God. It was from the spirit of defiance that confusion in the earth began, out of which came the emergence of national groups.

As each nation's consciousness has developed over the centuries (or for some countries, over the millennia), slowly a consensus idea has arisen for that set of people. That idea is both (1) "some standard of some activity" and (2) "concepts of [the] laws" of God. In this way, we might speak of "the spirit" of a nation—that is, what it aspires to and holds as its highest value.

America is presented as an illustration of this process. Although its national consciousness has had much less time to emerge than that of many other countries, Cayce suggests that one central value and aspiration is clearly observable: freedom. But inherent in that goal is the possibility for error or national fault. Since freedom is closely related to the spiritual attribute of free will, America is especially vulnerable to improper use of will. This can mean defiance—remember the primal fault that is described at the beginning of this reading.

But improper use of will also expresses in a more subtle way. Cayce asks us to think about the words of Jesus, "He shall know the truth and the truth then shall make him free." The key to freedom is in living and applying the truth in one's own life. The implication, then, is that Americans often fail to live the knowledge they have; they fail to live the truth. And what is that truth that frequently is forgotten and left unapplied? "In God We Trust."

This notion may leave Americans defensive. People all over the world fail to trust in God. Why is this universal tendency singled out as the significant fault of America? Simply because of what we have set as an aspiration. To hold freedom as a national ideal makes the proper use of will and right understanding of truth especially critical issues.

The reading goes on to identify the shortcomings or sins of other nations. Fewer details are offered than in the case of America. The national consciousness of England tends to hold the idea that they are a little bit better than others. The French err by an overindulgence of the body. The Italians fall into dissension (Cayce even offers a prayerful affirmation for that country that "a few might just agree, that a few even might declare their oneness with the higher forces"). The shortcoming of China has been its quiet isolation and self-satisfaction. And the sin of India has been to take knowledge and apply it exclusively in an inward way.

This reading also contains two of Cayce's most dramatic prophecies. One concerns Russia. That nation is depicted as the hope of the world, although not with its communistic system of government. Its leadership and positive influence is seen as concurrent with a friendly relation toward America. It's hard to say for sure if the accomplishments and good will initiated by Gorbachev's policy of glasnost is what Cayce had in mind. An earlier period of detente fell by the wayside, so there may be reason to be skeptical. But perhaps Cayce could perceive a broad spiritual trend, one that may have several false starts before the collective wills of Americans and Russians can make a new kind of relationship more permanent.

The second dramatic prediction relates to China—that it would one day be the cradle of Christianity (at least the application of its tenets, if not the doctrines of its churches). Are events of the late twentieth century the fulfillment of that prophecy, as the Chinese open themselves to Western ideas and lifestyle? Probably not. The reading was given in 1944, and although the timing Cayce had in mind is ambiguous, most likely fifty years doesn't qualify as "far off as man counts time." Even more extraordinary changes may well be in store for that country in the twenty-first century.

THE READING

This psychic reading, 3976-29, was given by Edgar Cayce on June 22, 1944, at the Thirteenth Annual A.R.E. Congress. The conductor was Gertrude Cayce.

[1]GC: It has been indicated through this channel that much might be given regarding what the vibrations of nations, as individuals, might mean. You will give such information concerning these vibrations and their relations to the spirit of the various nations, particularly in connection with the seven sins and twelve virtues in the human family, which will be helpful to us as an organization and as individuals in our attempt to be channels of blessing to our fellow men. You will then answer the questions, which may be submitted, as I ask them.

[2]EC: When there came about the periods of man's evolution in the earth, what was given then as to why man must be separated into tongues, into nations, into groups? "Lest they in their foolish wisdom defy God." What is here then intimated? That man, seeking his own gratification of the lusts of the flesh, might even in the earth defy God. With what, then, has man been endowed

by his Creator? All that would be necessary for each individual soul-entity to be a companion with God. And that is God's desire toward man.

[3]Thus when man began to defy God in the earth and the confusion arose which is represented in the Tower of Babel—these are representations of what was then the basis, the beginnings of nations. Nations were set up then in various portions of the land, and each group, one stronger than another, set about to seek their gratifications. Very few—yea, as ye will recall, it even became necessary that from one of these groups one individual, a man, be called. His ways were changed. His name was changed. Did it take sin away from the man, or was it only using that within the individual heart and purpose and desire even then, as man throughout the periods of unfoldment put—in his interpretation—that of material success first? It isn't that God chose to reserve or save anything that was good from man, so long as man was, is, and will be one who uses that living soul as a companion with God. That's God's purpose. That should be man's purpose.

[4]In the application of this principle, then, in the present day what has come about? Each nation has set some standard of some activity of man as its idea, either of man's keeping himself for himself or of those in such other nations as man's preparation for that companionship with God. For remember, there are unchangeable laws. For God is law. Law is God. Love is law. Love is God. There are then in the hearts, the minds of man, various concepts of these laws and as to where and to what they are applicable. Then, just as in the days of old, the nature of the flesh, human flesh and its natures, has not changed, but the spirit maketh alive. The truth maketh one free. Just as man has done throughout the ages, so in the present, as one takes those of the various nations as have seen the light and have, through one form or another, sought to establish as the idea of that nation, of

that people, some symbol that has and does represent those peoples in those days of the fathers of the present land called America.

[5]What is the spirit of America? Most individuals proudly boast "freedom." Freedom of what? When ye bind men's hearts and minds through various ways and manners, does it give them freedom of speech? Freedom of worship? Freedom from want? Not unless those basic principles are applicable throughout the tenets and lines as has been set, but with that principle freedom. For God meant man to be free and thus gave man will, a will even to defy God. *God* has not willed that any soul should perish, but hath with every trial or temptation prepared a way of escape.

[6]There have come through the various periods of man's unfoldment, teachers proclaiming "This the way, here the manner in which ye may know," and yet in the Teacher of Teachers is found the way, He who even in Himself fulfilled the law. For when God said, "Let there be light," there came Light into that which He had created, that was without form and was void and it became the Word, and the Word dwelt among men and men perceived it not. The Word today dwells among men and many men perceive it not.

[7]Those nations who have taken those vows that man shall be free should also take those vows "He shall know the truth and the truth then shall make him free."

[8]Then what is this that would be given thee today? Here is thy lesson: Hear ye all! Beware lest ye as an individual soul, a son, a daughter of God, fail in thy mission in the earth today; that those ye know, those ye contact shall know the truth of God, not by thy word, bombastic words, but in long-suffering, in patience, in harmony, that ye create in thine own lives, for it must begin with thee. God has shown thee the pattern, even one Jesus, who became the Christ that ye might have an advocate

with the Father, for the Father hath said "In the day ye eat or use the knowledge for thine own aggrandizement, ye shall die." But he that had persuaded the spirit, the souls that God had brought into being, to push into matter to gratify desire for self-expression, self-indulgence, self-satisfaction, said "Ye shall not surely die," or what were then the activities of man—for as had been said, "A day is a thousand years, a thousand years as a day."

[9]What was the length of life then? Nearly a thousand years. What is your life today? May it not be just as He had given, just as He indicated to those peoples, just as He did to the lawgiver, just as He did to David—first from a thousand years to a hundred and twenty, then to eighty? Why? Why? The sin of man in his desire for self-gratification.

[10]What nations of the earth today vibrate to those things that they have and are creating in their own land, their own environment? Look to the nations where the span of life has been extended from sixty to eight-four years. You will judge who is serving God. These are judgments. These are the signs to those who seek to know, who will study the heavens, who will analyze the elements, who will know the heart of man, they that seek to know the will of the Father for themselves answer "Lord, here am I, use me, send me where I am needed."

[11]Just as have been those principles of your present conflict. "Send help, for man's heritage of freedom will be taken away." By whom? He that hath said, "Surely ye will not die." There are those two principles, two conflicting forces in the earth today: the prince of this world, and that principle that says to every soul, "Fear not, I have overcome the world and the prince of the world hath nothing in me." Can ye say that? Ye must! That is thy hope; that "The prince of this world, Satan, that old serpent, hath no part in any desire of my mind, my heart, my body, that I do not control in the direction it shall

take." These are the things, these are the principles.

[12]What then of nations? In Russia there comes the hope of the world, not as that sometimes termed of the Communistic, of the Bolshevistic; no. But freedom, freedom! that each man will live for this fellow man! The principle has been born. It will take years for it to be crystallized, but out of Russia comes again the hope of the world. Guided by what? That friendship with the nation that hath even set on its present monetary unit "In God We Trust." (Do ye use that in thine own heart when you pay your just debts? Do ye use that in thy prayer when ye send thy missionaries to other lands? "I give it, for in God we trust"? Not for the other fifty cents either!)

[13]In the application of these principles, in those forms and manners in which the nations of the earth have and do measure to those in their activities, yea, to be sure, America may boast, but rather is that principle being forgotten when such is the case, and that is the sin of America.

[14]So in England, from whence have come the ideas—not ideals—ideas of being just a little bit better than the other fellow. Ye must *grow* to that in which ye will deserve to be known, deserve to receive. That has been, that is, the sin of England.

[15]As in France, to which this principle first appealed, to which then came that which was the gratifying of the desires of the body—that is the sin of France.

[16]In that nation which was first Rome, when there was that unfolding of those principles, its rise, its fall, what were they that caused the fall? The same as at Babel. The dissensions, the activities that would enforce upon these, in this or that sphere, servitude; that a few might just agree, that a few even might declare their oneness with the higher forces. For theirs was the way that seemeth right to a man but the end is death. That is the sin of Italy.

[17]The sin of China? Yea, there is the quietude that will not be turned aside, saving itself by the slow growth. There has been a growth, a stream through the land in ages which asks to be left alone to be just satisfied with that within itself. It awoke one day and cut its hair off! And it began to think and to do something with its thinking! This, here, will be one day the cradle of Christianity, as applied in the lives of men. Yea, it is far off as man counts time, but only a day in the heart of God—for tomorrow China will awake. Let each and every soul as they come to those understandings, do something, then, in his or her own heart.

[18]Just as in India, the cradle of knowledge not applied, except within self. What is the sin of India? *Self,* and left the "ish" off—just self.

[19]Then apply in thine own life truth. What is truth? It might have been answered, had an individual entity who stood at the crossways of the world waited for an answer. Yet that soul had purified itself and had given the new commandment that "ye love one another!"

[20]What is it all about then? "Thou shalt love the Lord thy God with all thine heart, thine soul, thine mind, thine body, and thy neighbor as thyself." The rest of all the theories that may be concocted by man are nothing, if these are just lived. Love thy neighbor as thyself in the associations day by day, preferring as did the Christ who died on the cross rather than preferring the world be His without a struggle.

[21]Know, then, that as He had His cross, so have you. May you take it with a smile. You can, if ye will let Him bear it with thee. Do it.

[22]We are through for the present.

PART TWO:
UNDERSTANDING THE JOURNEY OF THE SOUL

Chapter 5

USING YOUR SOUL TALENT

READING 4087-1

This reading is about child training, but it's also about the challenges that any of us face as we try to fulfill the potentials of our lives or help someone else do so. This reading is one of the best and most succinct examples of how reincarnation works. We can learn lessons about our own lives from its study, especially in regard to our talents.

The many life readings which Cayce gave for children are among the most fascinating case histories of his psychic work. There is something very special about a youngster like this six-year-old boy, whose parents turned to Cayce for help in 1944. A child such as he has a life that still stretches ahead with promise and possibility.

Distant past and upcoming future meet through Cayce's apparent ability to perceive clairvoyantly the deep patterns of the soul.

From background notes we know a little bit about this particular boy and why his parents sought help regarding child rearing. Several incidents had led them to believe that he was an unusual soul with a remarkable talent. The boy's innate psychic abilities made it evident that an interesting challenge lay ahead for the family:

how the boy could lead a normal life *and* fulfill the purpose for which his soul had chosen to be born now. The challenge was compounded by the fact that the parents were having troubles in their marriage. In fact, many of the paragraphs of the reading—especially 13 through 17—are directed to the parents rather than to the boy.

At the very start of this life reading, Cayce validates the reports of this boy's psychic experiences, indicating in paragraph 4 that in more than one past life he has had these abilities. There is even a brief description of how this operates within him to produce precognition ("visions of things to come") or clairvoyance ("things that are happening"). The triggering mechanism is the kundalini or life force rising spontaneously to the sixth spiritual center (pineal center) from the second center (what Cayce sometimes called the lyden center, associated with the cells of Leydig).

These spontaneous occurrences as a child were a way of visiting ancient patterns in his soul, especially related to the Old Testament era. Cayce describes a very specific past life, one that is even mentioned in the Bible (I Kings 13). A little background on the story helps us interpret Cayce's advice in paragraphs 5 through 8.

Nearly a thousand years before the birth of Christ and just after the death of King Solomon, Jeroboam successfully led a revolt in which the ten northern tribes established their own nation of Israel, with Jeroboam as the first king. Jeroboam, in an effort to keep his people from journeying to Jerusalem, set up local shrines. But many of them involved fostering cults alien to Judaism. It was against this practice that an unnamed prophet (the soul that was now this very boy, according to Cayce) confronted Jeroboam. Among the signs that he was an authentic spokesman of God, this prophet demonstrated an ability to wither the hand of the king and then to heal it.

The problem that arose for this prophet was *whom to*

trust. In his divinely inspired prophetic mission to confront Jeroboam, the prophet had also been given other
specific instructions. It was in regard to those instructions that he failed. A person also claiming to be a
prophet lied to him and persuaded him to disregard the
instructions—to his own undoing and violent death (see
I Kings 13: 15-25). This story is the source of Cayce's advice: " . . . he is not to listen at all of those who may counsel him as to the manner in which he is to use the
abilities . . . but [instead] to trust in Him who is the way."
Apparently there might still be the tendency within the
soul to be led astray with his psychic and spiritual gifts.

Cayce then refers to yet another lifetime in which this
soul demonstrated a tendency to misuse or misunderstand something about paranormal abilities. For a second time Cayce identifies the boy as the reincarnation of
a biblical character. Again it's a rather minor personage,
but a key player in a powerfully instructive story. (See
Acts 8:18-24 for the details of this account.) It involves a
man named Simon living in Samaria who desperately
wanted the power of laying-on-of-hands healing, as
demonstrated by Peter and John. He offers to buy from
Peter the ability—something that hits uncomfortably
close to home in our modern era of commercialism.
Cayce's comments in paragraph 10 refer to the lesson
learned by the soul in this encounter with Peter—a lesson about money and spiritual gifts that would be crucial for right use of his abilities in this lifetime.

What do these past-life stories given to a six year old
more than fifty years ago have to teach us today? Probably something about the right use of our own special
abilities. The same sort of process is at work for any of us
who have carried into the present lifetime some talent,
skill, or sensitivity from a previous incarnation. The talent need not be one as dramatic as visionary prophecies
or a lifetime as famous as some biblical character. The

principles of reincarnation, karma, and soul growth work the same way for everyone.

Attached to virtually any talent or strength within the soul is some challenge or temptation regarding how it will be used. Think of something at which *you* are talented. Maybe it's a skill with persuasion or finances or artistry. Perhaps it's an aptitude for understanding what other people are feeling or a knack for problem solving. No doubt that talent has a big role to play in the fulfillment of what you came to earth to do, just as psychic ability did for that six-year-old boy.

One key to your success at soul growth in this lifetime may be the same as for him: recognizing potential distortions or misapplications of that talent. It's not necessary to remember specific past lives. All we need to do is develop sensitivity to the patterns in our own souls, to see the little tugs and temptations that cross our paths whenever we start to use that talent. Cayce didn't mean to scare us (or that young boy) from using our special gifts. He just wanted us to keep in mind how any skill or talent can be a two-edged sword.

THE READING

This psychic reading, 4087-1, was given by Edgar Cayce on April 15, 1944. The conductor was Gertrude Cayce.

[1]GC: You will give the relations of this entity and the universe, and the universal forces; giving the conditions which are as personalities, latent and exhibited in the present life; also the former appearances in the earth plane, giving time, place and the name, and that in each life which built or retarded the development for the entity; giving the abilities of the present entity, that to which it may attain, and how. You will answer the questions, as I ask them:

²EC: Yes, we have the records here of that entity now known as or called [4087].

³As we find, there are great possibilities but there are also great problems to be met with the training and the direction for this entity through the formative years.

⁴For as we find this entity has more than once been among those who were gifted with what is sometimes called second sight, or the superactivity of the third eye. Whenever there is the opening, then, of the lyden (Leydig) center and the kundaline forces from along the pineal, we find that there are visions of things to come, of things that are happening.

⁵Yet in the use of these through some experiences, as we will find, the entity is in the present meeting itself. For the entity was the prophet who warned Jeroboam. Read it! You will see why he is not to listen at all of those who may counsel him as to the manner in which he is to use the abilities that have been and are a portion of the entity's experience; but to trust in Him who is the way.

⁶Do not get away from the church! In the church keep these activities, that there may be surety in self that has to do or to deal with only the use of such insight, such vision, to the glory of the Father as manifested in the Son.

⁷Do not use such for gratifying, satisfying, or even encouraging the entity to use such. But do train the entity in the use of divine purpose, divine desire. For if the purpose and the desire is right, we may find that the entity may—as in the experience before this—use the activities for the benefit of his fellow man.

⁸For in the use of the power that has been a portion of the entity's consciousness there may come help to many.

⁹For in the experience before this the entity attempted to buy same from Peter. Hence that tendency, that realization that the misuse of same may bring destructive forces into the experience.

¹⁰In that experience the entity being warned, as he

asked "Pray that I may be forgiven for the thought that such might be purchased," he was forgiven. For as it was indicated, "What thou shalt bind on earth shall be bound in heaven, what thou shalt loose on earth shall be loosed in heaven." There we find that the entity through that experience used the ability granted through such for a greater understanding, a greater interpretation. For all of God that any individual may know is already within self. It is in the application and the practice of same within self, in its relations to its desires, its hopes, its fears, and to its fellow man. For as ye sow, ye must reap.

[11]Before that the entity was the prophet of Judah who was sent to Jeroboam to warn him, and who brought about the withering of the hand, and also the healing of same; yet turned aside when faced with that in which the mind said "A more excellent way."

[12]There are no shortcuts. What God hath commanded is true. For the law of the Lord is perfect and it converteth the soul.

[13]Here the parents have a real, real obligation. They have a real, real opportunity. So live in self that thine own lives may be an example to this entity through its formative years. So teach, not let it be given to someone else— so teach, for it is thy responsibility, not the priest's, not a teacher's, *not* a minister's responsibility, but thine. Don't put it off. Don't neglect, or else ye will meet self again.

[14]In the training let it first begin with self, as with the entity [4087]. Joseph he should be called. Let the training begin with that indicated in Exodus 19:5—"If thou will harken to the voice, He hath a special work, a special mission for thee—but thou must harken to the voice within, that ye present thy body as a living sacrifice, holy and acceptable unto Him, which is a reasonable service." For they who have been called, who have been ordained to be messengers have the greater responsibility; not as a saint—for there is more joy in heaven over one sinner

than ninety and nine who are so-called saints, or those who are themselves satisfied with that they do.

[15]Then study that interpreted in Romans. Ye will find it is not from somewhere else, not from out of the blue, not from overseas, not from before the altar. For thy body is indeed the temple and there he may indeed meet his Maker. There indeed may he meet himself. There indeed may he open the door of his own consciousness so that the Master may walk and talk with him.

[16]Do not discourage, do not encourage the visions—until the first lessons are learned.

[17]Then there will be the needs that *thou,* as well as others, take heed to the warnings this entity may be sent to give.

[18]We are through for the present.

Chapter 6

THE MIND OF THE SOUL

READINGS 3744-1 AND 3744-2

These readings provide an in-depth statement about the nature of the mind with special reference to the soul and the mind of the soul. It's a good example of just how specific and comprehensive the Cayce source could be in responding to thoughtful questions about the nature of reality. Although the language is sometimes difficult to understand, many significant principles are clearly identifiable.

What functions does mind play? More than merely intellectual thought. This reading uses such words as "storehouse" (i.e., memory), "reasons" (both deductively and inductively), "segregates," "correlates," and "divides" to portray its diverse activity. As the reading puts it, mind is an "active force."

Mind is depicted as a process that goes on between various forces of our being and the world. The phrase used is "the factor governing . . . the interlaying space . . . between." For example, the conscious mind is largely the product of what goes on between the senses of the physical body on the one hand and the material world on the other. As sensory-deprivation research has shown, when we remove impressions coming from the physical environment, then normal waking consciousness is likely to shift to an altered state of awareness.

The subconscious mind is largely created by the interaction of soul forces and spiritual forces. As we see in one of the later answers, each soul is an individualized creation of God, having its own free will, and inherently motivated to seek for unity with its Maker. The subconscious mind—one aspect of the unconscious—can be thought of as the mind of the soul itself.

One of the most intriguing qualities of the mind is the way in which suggestion works. Suggestions can include words spoken to us by a friend, statements we hear on television commercials, thoughts we focus on as a meditation affirmation, and dozens of other possibilities. The conscious mind perceives a suggestion and it stimulates similar thoughts and recent memories ("Suggestion to the conscious mind only brings to the mental plane, those forces that are of the same character . . .").

But the same suggestion is also perceived by the mind of the soul—the subconscious. Here the response is more complicated because other forces come into play. Now the direction and impact of the suggestion "may be waved" by unseen factors. Suggestions to the subconscious are influenced by deep soul memories (which differ from individual to individual) and by the universal forces themselves. One application of this principle would seem to be that we cannot manipulate the unconscious aspects of the mind quite as easily as we might think.

Cayce's view of the mind is elaborate and comprehensive. Some people who have not studied the readings carefully have assumed that the useful phrase "Mind is the builder" is about all he had to say on the matter. But these excerpts should prove otherwise. We should also remember that all the readings were not given at the same time, and that we can observe a certain development of some of these ideas. For example, in this 3744 series the subconscious mind is described as "lying between the soul and spirit forces." Years later in reading 900-21 the source of this information seems to have altered terminology saying, "The superconscious [is] the divide, that oneness lying between the soul and the spirit force . . . "

Yet in spite of evolving definitions or language patterns that are difficult to follow, Cayce's description of the mind is noteworthy for the way it integrates psychology and spirituality. It challenges us to turn many of our preconceived notions upside down. It invites us to recognize the active presence of a mind of the soul.

THE READINGS

This is a composite of readings 3744-1 and 3744-2, given on consecutive days in 1923. They were part of a series given in the first year that Cayce's repertoire expanded beyond health diagnosis to virtually any topic. Cayce's secretary, Gladys Davis, explained that the questions and answers in this series were "rearranged under topics, so that we later could not tell which questions were asked and answered in which readings." The 3744 series forms the basis for all subsequent questioning through the readings along metaphysical lines. This part began with Mr. Cayce being asked to define the word "mind":

That which is the active force in an animate object; that is the spark, or image of the Maker. Mind is the factor that is in direct opposition of will. Mind being that control of, or being the spark of the Maker, the *will*, the individual when we reach the plane of man. Mind being and is the factor governing the contention, or the interlaying space, if you please, between the physical to the soul, and the soul to the spirit forces within the individual or animate forces. We have the manifestation of this within the lowest order of animal creation. These are developed as the mind is developed, both by the action of all of the senses of the body, as we have them developed in man. *Mind* is *that* that reasons the impressions from the senses, as they manifest before the individual.

The active principle that governs man. Mind a factor, as the senses are of the mind, and as the soul and spirit are factors of the entity, one in all, all in one. We are speaking from the normal plane, of course. As the impressions are reached to the storehouse of the body, the mind is that factor, that principle, that portion that either segregates, correlates or divides the impression to the portion needed, to develop the entity or physical force toward the spark or infinite force, giving the life force to the body. The mind may be classified into the two forces—that between the physical and soul, and that between the soul and spirit force. We see the manifestations of this, rather than the object or the mind itself. We find this always manifested through one of the senses, the same as we find the psychic forces a manifestation of the soul and spirit; the *mind* a manifestation of the physical.

With the division of the mind force as given, we see why in the physical plane individuals become misunderstood or misrepresented. They do not reach the same manifestations from other individuals. Hence the expression, "They are all of one mind." "To *do good*, they become of one mind, *to do evil* they are many." The nearer approach the mind comes to the divide, between the soul and spirit forces, the nearer we become to that infinite force that guides when it is allowed to the individual's actions day by day.

Definition of the words "conscious mind":

The *conscious* means *that* that is able to be manifested in the physical plane through one of the senses.

Definition of the word "subconscious mind":

That lying between the soul and spirit forces within the entity, and is reached more thoroughly when the conscious mind is under subjugation of the soul forces of the individual or physical body. We may see manifestation in those of the so-called spiritual-minded people. The manifestation of the subconscious in their action. That portion of the body, better known as the one that propagates or takes care of the body—physical, mental, moral or whatnot, when it is not able to take care of itself.

Subconscious is *unconscious* force. This may be seen in every nerve end, in every muscular force. Subconscious action may be brought into manifestation by the continual doing of certain acts in the physical plane, so the body becomes unconscious of doing the acts that it does.

(Q) How can we best develop our subconscious minds to be of the most benefit to our fellow men while in the physical plane of living?

(A) By developing the mental or physical mind toward the uplift of mankind toward the Maker, leaving those things behind that so easily beset the physical body. By the training of the mental, through physical force, the subconscious urge, as we have given, the faculty of doing in the right or direct way, and lending assistance to the uplift of all.

The *thought* held against an individual directs the mind either of masses or classes, whether toward good or bad.

Thought is reached through the physical forces, and by becoming a part of the physical or conscious mind either lends the strength of subconscious forces or allows the subconscious to direct. Not that the physical mind gives strength, but by allowing the subconscious to direct, and not building the barrier between to be overcome.

That to be overcome might as well be met in this plane, for it will have to be met before we can gain the entrance to the Holy of Holies. This is the manner in which to train or conduct the physical to lend the assistance to the subconscious forces to direct and give the help the world or populace needs.

(Q) Mr. Cayce, what is the soul of a body?

(A) That which the Maker gave to every entity or individual in the beginning, and which is seeking the home again or place of the Maker.

(Q) Does the soul ever die?

(A) May be banished from the Maker, not death.

(Q) What is the subconscience [subconscious?] mind of the body?

(A) An attribute of the soul.

(Q) What is the difference in suggestion to the subconscious mind and the conscious mind?

(A) Suggestion to the conscious mind only brings to the mental plane, those forces that are of the same character and the conscious is the suggestion action. In that of suggestion to the subconscious mind gives its reflection or reaction from the universal forces or mind or superconscious forces . . .

By the suggestion just as given may be waved [waived?] by the forces that are brought to bear on the subconscious to reach the conscious mind, just as we have in a purely mechanical form. Any object or wood, especially, projected into water appears bended; just so with the reflection from suggestions to the subconscious to reach the conscious or mental forces appear bended in their action or in the manifestation of their action to the physical or conscious forces of individuals.

(Q) Just what is meant by force and forces?

(A) Depending upon the conditions under which incentive or that, which is being acted upon and that which is acting. As we have in the body of a living physical being, we have a body made up of many atoms, and their relation to each other depends upon the force as is given in each part to work upon or in or through the system. In the nerve system we find that of the force of physical matter or subconscious or soul matter, of superconscious or spirit matter, all receiving a force, as illustrated, we would have it here: When any object or injury comes to a portion of the body, then the nerves transmit that to the physical or conscious brain to be removed; the forces of all of the elementals or that is, of the parts of the body are brought into play; that which carries, that which replenishes, that which comes, that is force or forces, as may be. Or as we would have in the one word to express all force: That which is the spirit of any object, whether animate or inanimate, physical or material, that of the Divine, which carries all force. We only have to take into consideration, but the relativity of the condition, position, time, place as to which or what element of force is implied in giving the elements of force from the subconscious force to the conscious force. In this also we may see how the correct reflection may appear bended.

(Q) Is it possible for this body, Edgar Cayce, in this state to communicate with anyone who has passed into the spirit world?

(A) The spirit of all that have passed from the physical plane remain about the plane until their development carry them onward or are returned for their development here. When they are in the plane of communication or remain within this sphere, any may be communicated with. There are thousands about us here at present.

(Q) In the subconscious giving this information when in this state, how are we to know on the physical plane from whence and from which condition it gives this information?

(A) Just as we know as to the force implied from whatever element the force is given, we must know from that force the information is obtained, deflected only by the expression of the individual, whom obtains the information, by the results obtained in the end. Just as we have in the diagnosis is for the betterment or advancement of the individual, just as the subconscious that communicates to the physical for with the physical submerged, a universal condition. It may be obtained from all or in part, just as needs for the individual. None is gained from one individual, but as there are good personages, there are good individuals, not necessarily within the same manifested body—just so in the spirit force there are good and there are bad personages still reflected. As these give rise to the expression and all give expression of experience of themselves of the entity through which the information is obtained gives that deflection as we may find with the surroundings of those not good, we will find the results in the same. Results in diagnosis give of the forces whether from the spirit forces are good or material forces are good, then judge. Just as the seed of truth is ever the same, and its productions are ever by the same, though some may fall in fallow land or some may fall in stony land.

(Q) What is meant by the banishment of a soul? from its Maker?

(A) Of the will as given in the beginning to choose for self, as in the earthly plane, all insufficient matter is cast onto Saturn. To work out its own salvation as would be termed in the word, the entity or individual banishes itself or its soul, which is its entity.

(Q) What is meant by the re-entering of the personel [personality?] as in the beginning?

(A) The personel [personality?] is that as known on the physical plan when in the subconscious or when the subconscious controls, the personel [personality?] is removed from the individual, and only that of the other forces in the Trinity occupies the body and use only its elements to communicate as in this body here, as we have spoken of. With the submerging of the conscious to the subconscious or superconscious, the personel [personality?] of the body or earthly portions are removed and lie above the other body. They may be seen here, hence the distributing of those conditions brings distress to the other portions of the entity or individual. With the return then we find the personel [personality?] leaves those impressions with those portions of the body, as we have given for the arm force here, you see.

(Q) To what place or state does the subconscious pass to receive this information it gives?

(A) Just here in the same sphere as when the spirit or soul or spirit and soul are driven or removed from the body or person.

(Q) What is meant by aliments [ailments? elements?] of the soul, mental and spiritual forces on which this work may border?

(A) Mental is of the physical, which with its relative forces connecting the soul force and unbalancing of the trugh [truth?] may perform on the soul forces that which brings abnormal results to physical and soul matter. The correction of these only means that it, the work, assists the individual or the entity to find itself and to follow in that way that would lead that individual to its own better self. Each individual must leads its own life, whether in this sphere or in the other planes . . .

Chapter 7

Soul Development

READING 696-3

This deep, complex reading is rich in principles about soul development. The source of the material addresses the *soul mind* of the recipient. The ideas in this reading seemed so significant that excerpts were sent to the original "A Search for God" group that was compiling lesson essays on the destiny of the body, mind, and soul.

Beginning with the role of the mind in soul development, it describes what the mind needs to eliminate—"less of self" and "less of the personal desires"—to foster soul growth. We might interpret this to mean a willingness to let go of our own personal agendas—the projects and plans that we are compulsively driven to attain. Later in the reading, this same tendency is presented as an exclusive attention to one's own desires and needs ("when ye cry for *self*, and *self* alone, ye close the door").

The reading goes on to describe specific qualities associated with an inner path of growth. One is a *feeling* or an *emotion* that comes from our spiritual nature. This is a subtle point that shouldn't be missed. Feelings don't come only from the senses. Emotions aren't exclusively linked to the body. There are higher emotions—feelings of the spirit—and a mind that is intent on soul development will experience them.

Another significant ingredient for soul development is hope, which is defined here as "the expectancy of the inner self." At first, this definition may strike us as inappropriate. We've learned the hard way that expectations often lead to disappointment. If we expect too much—hoping for the impossible—we're likely to suffer a big letdown. What does the likelihood of disappointment have to do with soul development?

The key to understanding what Cayce means is in the distinction between "expectancy" and "expectations." The latter term usually means something quite specific: a condition or material manifestation that one desires. For example, we might have expectations of a physical healing by a certain date or an employment offer from a particular company. On the other hand, expectancy is an openness to receive. It's an inner knowing that one's own sincere efforts coupled with assistance from higher sources will produce something that will be exactly what's needed. Expectancy—that is, hope—is being joyfully ready to meet life and all it has to offer.

Patience is yet another quality that is essential to soul development. It's described in the opening paragraph as the mirror opposite to personal desire. As we are patient we can then become *aware* of the longings of our own soul-self. The clear implication here is that we're usually unconscious of these desires of the higher self.

Another side of patience as a key to soul development is found in the answer to the first question, a profound inquiry about the challenge to do the right thing in spite of opposing worldly influences. Here Cayce defines patience as "seeing all time as *one* time." Past, present, and future are inherently connected. This is not the same thing as saying that there is no such thing as time. Instead, it's an invitation to see difficulties in material life from a new perspective and to let go of fear. In fact, both patience and hope are powerful antidotes to that crippling emotion. With the soul development that comes through patience and hope we find that "less do the things of the earth cause fear."

A theme that runs through this reading is *expression*. The implication is that soul development is tied to manifestation or expression of our inner nature. The idea comes up several times in this reading, with slightly different phrases:

"the more, then, that thy soul is in expression";

"the power comes in giving the expression of the inner self";

"to thine own soul's best expression."

One example of such soul expression that is mentioned on multiple occasions is *the awakening of hope in others*. There is something about such efforts—to stimulate in other people a sense of hope and expectancy—that is particularly related to our *own soul* development.

Finally, it's important to note how the reading ends—not the final words of the answer to the last question, but the conclusion of the opening discourse. In many readings, Cayce's source saved a significant principle for the ending of the opening discourse. In this reading it's: "Put thy trust, thy faith, thy hope, in thy soul!" We're used to hearing admonitions to trust God, but do we also remember to trust ourselves? Could it be that along with all the essential ingredients needed for soul development (e.g., higher emotions, hope, patience), self-trust is just as important? We must realize that it's not just any "self" that is referred to. Trust your soul. Trust your inner self, and in so doing you'll find that that soul-self grows and develops even further.

THE READING

This psychic reading, 696-3, was given by Edgar Cayce January 28, 1935. The conductor was Gertrude Cayce.

[1]GC: You will have before you the body and enquiring mind of [696] present in this room, who seeks information, counsel and guidance as to her best mental and spiritual development. You will give that which will be of most help to her at this time, answering the questions she submits as I ask them.

[2]EC: Yes, we have the body, the enquiring mind, the *soul* mind, of the entity known as or called [696].

[3]In giving that which may be helpful at this time, consider that which is necessary for the soul development. While the mind, as it is commonly spoken of, is the builder, it—as the personality and individuality of an entity—has two phases. The mind functions irrespective of the body. Hence that which is builded for the development of the soul body is for expression of the soul mind, or superconscious mind—that is as the mental mind, or that may be trained in a physical body as to care for same. Hence more and more that the mind in its activity is of the soul's development, the less and less of self is expressed and more and more the consciousness, the awareness, of a condition, an event, a feeling, an emotion, an expression that deals with the attributes of the soul-body. So does the soul become aware of the presence of the creative conscience, the oneness of self in that which is the essence of life itself. When there is less and less of the personal desires, more and more does *patience* become a portion of the whole being—and the awareness of the soul's longings, the soul's desires, the soul's expressions of Him in *true,* pure love. When those things of the mental mind—that have to do with the body—come as distresses, anxieties, hurts, pains, these

are of the body-conscience, and are the self, the ego, of that which is the expression of the soul. For as may be given in material surroundings, when an individual has a friend that is lovely to Him, to make other friendships does not lessen the love for the other. Should there enter jealousy, doubt, fear as to the place in the individual's own heart or mind being supplanted, these are physical; these are selfishness in their manifestations. For when the soul is in its manifestations it is as God so loved the world, even those that hated Him, even those that put Him oft to shame, even those that called on other gods, even those that made a companion of Satan—the emissaries that are in direct opposition to the Christ Consciousness, even these—God so loved that He gave Himself, His Son, that we, His children, His brethren of the Christ, might—through the Christ—have the greater access to the Father. So, in thy seeking let thy soul—that is in Him—ever, day by day, find the greater expression. And in this expression does there come the more and more awareness of what hope is, as the expectancy of the inner self. For, as expressed by Him, there is *joy* in heaven, in the presence of the Father, when individuals within their inner selves open their souls to the Father, that He may—as the sacrifice was given—know the beauty of that sacrifice was not in vain. So, by this opening of the soul, the entity may find the essence of faith in Him to keep His promises. Even though the heavens fall, even though the earth and all the pleasures and the joy of earth be rolled up, His promises shall not fail. And those in faith are righteousness, and the hope becomes glorified and the soul becomes more and more aware; and less do the things of earth cause fear or trembling, or even wonderment save at the joys that are preserved in the promises of the Son, of the Father, to those that love Him.

[4]The more, then, that thy soul is in expression as ye give to thy fellow man in word, in act, in association, that

which arouses hope and faith such that it takes hold upon the superconscious mind, the more is there the oneness of the soul in Him. For when ye worry about this or that activity of individuals in the earth, and their words, their deeds, their acts, even of those that ye in your body-mind may love, may worship, these may become as lepers to thy soul. Put thy trust, thy faith, thy hope, in thy soul!

[5]Ready for questions.

[6](Q) The thought of what others consider right will enter in even when one knows deep within that he is gaining great soul development from actions whose high motives are not seen and understood from the outside world. When one's inner self repeatedly dictates a course which the world perhaps would misunderstand, how can one bravely follow that inner dictate and be free from the fear of misunderstanding. Give me a passage of scripture or a message to strengthen me.

(A) The passage is, "My Spirit—(thy soul)—beareth witness with thy spirit as to whether ye be truly the sons and daughters of God or not." Not merely conscience, but *do* all things for conscience's sake, that there may be harmony in thine inner self. Or, would that all would learn that He, the Christ Consciousness, is the Giver, the Maker, the Creator of the world and all that be therein! And ye are His, for ye are bought with a price, even that of passing through flesh as thou that He might experience and know all thy thoughts, thy fears, thy shortcomings, thy desires, the dictates of the physical consciousness, the longings of the physical body. Yet He is at the right hand, *is* the right hand, *is* the intercessor for ye all. Hence thy destinies lie in Him. And again, as the scripture hath said, "God hath not willed that any soul should perish, or that any should be cut off from His face, but hath with the temptation prepared a way of escape." Hence the *necessity* of patience, of living in the soul, seeing all time as *one* time, that ye may know whereunto thou hast been called. And though thy brother, thy friend, thy dearest one finds fault or becomes discouraged because he is going his own way, if thou wilt call—His promise has been, "Though ye wander far afield, though ye be forsaken, though ye be misunderstood, if ye will call I will hear!" And if ye be on the Lord's side, *who* can be against you?

⁷(Q) What is my specific work with the Association for Research and Enlightenment, and how can I best carry it out?

(A) Presenting the spiritual truths to thy fellow man, to the world, that are presented through its lessons, its messages, individual and collective, that others may take hope. For, as thou hast from thine own experiences in the earth known the more oft the seeking to present the law, the love (for law and love must be in their essence of the same source), and as thou hast *defended*—as thou hast presented such to thy self-centered, wayward brethren here and there, then present them again and again. How oft shall I forgive my brother? Seven times? Yea, seventy times seven! How oft shall ye present the lessons? Seven? Yea, seventy times seven, that His way may be had among men! His *glory* is *present. See* the Savior as He is!

⁸(Q) Convinced that my present life's work is inspirational writing, I desire to know what specific course I should follow in life in order to gain more experience which will give me further deep insight into my fellow man's needs.

(A) As illustrated by that given, the power comes in giving the expression of the inner self, letting the soul manifest, letting the self—the personality of self—become less and less in its desires, letting His desire be the ruling force. As He gave out, so was the power, the ability, the experience His that He *is*, He *was*, He *ever will be* the expression, the *concrete* expression of *love* in the minds, the hearts, the souls of men.

Then, broaden thy field of activity. Fear not to approach thy observations in columns even of the secular world; as the *Christian Herald* or *Christian Advocate,* or the *Sunday School Times.* For the more and more that ye have the body of many giving praises and thanks for the hope that ye create in their minds and their hearts, greater is the experience and the *ability* of expression. For the law, the love holds as He gave; one may cry aloud and long for *self* and yet *never* be heard, but where two or three are gathered in His name there is He in the midst of them. So, as ye give out is the power received. Do not understand that ye may not enter into thine own closet and there meet thy Savior within, but—as given—when ye cry for *self,* and *self* alone, ye close the door, ye stand as a shadow before the altar of thy god within thyself.

Give, then, in broader fields of activity, in *every* channel where those that are seeking may find; that are wandering, that are lame in body, lame in mind, halt in their manner of expression, that are blind to the beauties in their own household, their own hearts, their own minds. These thou may awaken in all thy fields. And as ye do, greater is thy vision—and He will guide thee, for He hath given His angels charge concerning those that seek to be a channel of blessing to their fellow man; that purge their hearts, their bodies, of every selfish motive and give the Christ—*crucified, glorified*—a place in its stead.

[9](Q) Is Washington the best location for me?

(A) In the present. And as it is in the present the center, the hope as it were of the present civilization, so may it radiate to all portions even of the earth in that thou may be the representative of the Father-Son *in* that hope to many peoples everywhere!

[10](Q) Are my present living conditions such as will promote this insight and further my own soul growth?

(A) These, as we find, clarify themselves *of* themselves as the better self puts that it comprehends and understands *into* operative forces *in* the minds and hearts of others. This situation, then, purifies itself—even as running, living water. The debris, the harmful things, the conditions that would hinder are brushed aside as the life, the expressions of self are given out.

[11](Q) What is my spiritual duty toward Marvin and how can I best discharge it? Are we thrown into contact because of past karmic conditions? How can I further his spiritual awakening?

(A) As the magnet draws the compass that would direct or diverge the paths of those that sail upon life's seas. There are those individuals whose lives and thine own have made and do make for those things that are as whettingstones for the keenness of expression, the sharpness of the drawing of the perspective, or the dulling of the aches and pains that come from the shocks of contact with materiality in thine study into spiritual realms. These have their place. So has this association its place. But let it ever be as a *help* for self. For, as has been given by the poet, when thou are true to that which calls and answers within thee to thine own soul's best expression, thou wilt not be false to any, in any need which a soul may have! For ye are—are ye not all children of the one God! Are ye not brethren with the one purpose! And who shall gainsay that thou may not save a soul from stumbling over itself?

Keep thy head erect, thine purpose set, the Christ thy pilot, the magnet that draws thee His love!

[12]We are through for the present.

Chapter 8

"Neither Do I Condemn Thee . . . "

READING 479-1

Self-condemnation, the subject of this unusual physical reading, is a potent negative force. When we turn upon ourselves, we disturb the expression of life itself and interrupt our connection to what makes life meaningful. That principle is made clear in the first paragraph of what Gladys Davis (Mr. Cayce's secretary) referred to as "like no other physical reading."

The twenty-one-year-old recipient suffered from considerable unhappiness due to his homosexuality. In fact, it was a friend who wrote to Mr. Cayce to request help, saying: "He can't adapt himself to his condition and can't understand it. His condition, as I see it, is something that is no fault of his own, but is something that seems to be inborn in his nature. He doesn't understand what to do . . . And, as long as he has to stay in the state that he is in, his life will be nothing but misery . . . Why, this trouble that he has, has made him lose all faith in everything—absolutely everything. And I think that if you can help him adjust himself to his condition it will be as great and as important as any other case that you have helped."

Cayce's reading is an inspiring and impassioned call for this young man to move beyond the crippling influence of self-criticism. The message here is relevant to virtually everyone, since most of us are hindered to some degree by self-judgment.

In paragraph 4, Cayce shows us how to move beyond self-condemnation. Though we usually blame or judge ourselves for our shortcomings, from a higher perspective, these elements in our lives are *gifts*, opportunities through which real soul growth can emerge. And so, what is "often counted as sin or error" can be seen as a challenge—something initiated by an omniscient and loving Creator who has purposefully set up this chance for learning and development. It's such a prominent theme to this reading that the closing paragraph even comes back to it: ". . . that which has *seemed* to be to thee as a hindrance [may] become a steppingstone to the glory of thine own soul!"

Cayce's insightful point of view about our weaknesses *isn't* a clever attempt to rationalize them away or blame them on God. We still need to take responsibility for ourselves. Nor is this philosophy one that denies the reality of error or sin (read carefully paragraph 10 to see how seriously Cayce takes the reality of darkness and ungodliness). However, we can look at ourselves with loving eyes and believe that spiritual guidance has played a role shaping the difficulties, challenges, and shortcomings we face. It's a privilege to work under the tension of a handicap, Cayce suggests in paragraph 5.

One misconception we need to shed is any imagined link between the genuine virtue of humility and harsh self-judgment. Superficially it might seem that putting oneself down is a first step toward selflessness, but Cayce warns that *any* kind of condemnation is a "selfish manifestation."

Think of self-condemnation in terms of two aspects of oneself—that is, two sub-personalities, as psychology sometimes calls them. One sub-personality is "the con-

demned" and the other sub-personality is "the con-
demner." That accusatory self claims a kind of selfish
superiority, standing in haughty judgment. Of course,
what we *experience* most acutely in self-condemnation
is the emotional pain and the paralysis which belong to
the condemned self. It's no fun to be put down, even by
oneself. But in this tangled web of sub-personalities, we
need to recognize that something selfish is going on—
self-inflation. Perhaps that's why Cayce's psychology so
often links self-aggrandizement and self-condemnation,
describing them as the two fundamental flaws of our inner, mental life.

Cayce's solution, in paragraphs 7 and 8, offers the
hopeful promise that powerful forces can help us deal
with this problem. Our relationship to the redeeming
Christ is the key to moving out of the vicious cycle of self-
aggrandizement and self-condemnation. It's the "graciousness of the Christ spirit" that makes possible an
overcoming. And to emphasize what a model Christ is
for us, Cayce points us to Jesus' words, "Neither do I condemn thee, but sin no more."

That's precisely how we're called upon to treat ourselves—to refrain from paralyzing self-judgment and
also to challenge ourselves to do our very best next time.
We need to apply this philosophy when we catch ourselves doing less than the best. Do we look back with re-
gret, blame, and self-condemnation? Do we berate
ourselves, spending days, weeks, or months second-
guessing what we should have done, or feeling guilty? Of
course, some measure of retrospection is valuable, but it
needs to be brief and without self-criticism.

The next step is to look ahead. Ask yourself, "How do I
intend to act next time this situation arises?" That hopeful, forward-looking attitude is the gift of the Spirit to
ourselves. When we recognize our shortcomings but are
eager to do it better, we can be sure we're on track with

precisely what this reading called us all to do.

THE READING

This psychic reading, 479-1, was given by Edgar Cayce on January 6, 1934. The conductor was Gertrude Cayce.

(Physical Suggestion)

[1]EC: Yes, we have the body and those conditions physical and mental that disturb the better manifestations of life and its meaning through the physical forces as manifested in this body.

[2]Now, as we find, in giving the physical conditions that may be aided in bringing about for the body better manifestations, it would be rather the analyses of the conditions physical and mental that confront the body, or that must be met by the body.

[3]That there are physical defects in the structural portion, or in apparent manifestations through the mental, that are prenatal in their basic forces is too often condemned by the entity—and if there is the proper understanding of that which is Life in a manifestation, and the spiritual force that prompts the activity of same, these may be *by all* better understood.

[4]For, when there are those activities in a material world that bring about the forces or influences wherein there may be the action of a soul in its development, that which is often counted as sin or error is for the mercy to a soul from an All-Wise and beneficent Father that is directing, planning, giving the soul an opportunity for the use of that which may come into the experience *of* that soul in the material plane. And what the soul, through its body and mind and attributes of same, does about the knowledge and consciousness of the indwelling of the spirit of life through the Christ in the earth is the opportunity for that soul to develop.

[5]Hence in this particular body, rather than condemning, rather than closing self to the abilities in self or the opportunities wherein there may be made manifest in self that there is no condemning, but rather that self may use the opportunity, the privilege, to manifest under handicap or under those conditions that are existent within self—for the better manifesting of the love that is shed among men, through the activities in any one experience or environ.

[6]For, when a soul, a body-mind, a consciousness *condemns,* it is but a selfish manifestation—and is the attempt, as of the first errors, to *blame* that self has to do upon another.

[7]But if the soul will but know that the love of the Father (that has been manifested through His Son, who overcame sin, error, dis-ease, disease and even death itself in the material plane) has promised that through the consciousness of that life of the Christ awakening within us, as the consciousness of His indwelling presence, it may bring also healing in His wings, and that which had apparently been a hindrance may come to be the measure through which others may come to have the greater knowledge, the greater understanding of the Christ Consciousness, the Christ Life in the own experience, then all material problems will be understood and overcome.

[8]And rather than shutting self away from associates or companionship, if the consciousness will but make for the fruits of the spirit of the Christ being manifest, there will be the seeking on the part of others to *be near,* to be in the light of that which may be shed abroad by such a soul, in such a body making manifest in this mundane sphere that love, that life, that graciousness of the Christ spirit in the life.

[9]Hence, as we would find, if the body will thus find in self and in self's experience, there may come that *cleansing* within the physical forces of the body that will *make*

the body-*soul* whole indeed!

[10]Hence, *seek* to know *His* ways with thee. Not alone by denying that sin or error exists. *True,* sin and error is not of *God*—save through His sons that *brought* error, through selfishness, into the experience of the souls of men, the body by which angels and archangels are separate from the fullness of the Father. For, in His mercy He has given to all that which is the desire of every heart in a material plane—to seek companionship in a manner that there may be the exchange of experiences in whatsoever sphere the body-soul may find self. And in so doing, if there is the manifestation of greed, avarice, hate, selfishnesses, unkindliness, ungodliness, it makes for the harkenings that bring their fruit—contention, strife, hate, avarice, and separation from the light. For, those that have turned their face *from* the light of God can only see shadow or darkness and that light is only for those far away. Yet, if the soul will but turn to the Father of love as manifested in the earth through the Christ, in this life also may there be seen the light and the glory of a *new* birth.

[11]That all have been conceived in sin is only a partial truth; hence often makes a whole lie to those that in the body find their own physical selves may find that which to their own consciousness they can condemn in another. But to condemn—even as the Master taught when the moral laws, or when the physical laws or spiritual laws were being broken and were presented to Him as examples whereunto they would question Him, He always answered: "Thou hast no power over me save it be given thee from the Father, who has not left His children alone but ever seeks that they should know that the Redeemer liveth." And His light, His life, His love, *cleanseth* every *whit!* And, as He said unto the woman, "Neither do I condemn thee, but sin no more." Neither did He set for her any moral law but that which was conscious within

her own soul as to the acts in the physical that would tend to separate or to turn the light into darkness in the life of that soul. And as she came to be known among those that had sought the light, her life became that which led many to an understanding—and still will bring life, light and comprehension to many.

[12]So in thine own self, know that *therein* lies the spirit of God—the *soul* of thine self. The spirit will quicken, if the soul will but acknowledge His power, His divine right *within* thee!

[13]Then, let the acts of thine body, the temple of thine soul, be kept clean in thine own consciousness even as the presence of the Master cleansed every body that sought aid from physical dis-ease or corruption and made for the manifesting of the fruits of the spirit, of truth in their lives. Not that it saved the *body* from the grave, not that it saved a body from its transition from one sphere to another—but *quickened* rather the soul and *its* mind to such a degree that it would ever cry as did the Master in His message of old to His peoples that had been led through the trials and tribulations, "Others may do as they may, but as for me I—my soul, my body, my mind—will serve the *living* God!" [Josh. 24:15]

[14]Blessed is he whom the Lord chasteneth, for He loveth every one—and will quicken those that call on His name and act in accordance with the directions that are given every soul to know to do good and to do it not becomes sin, but to know that He—the Christ—will stand within thy stead and will cleanse the soul-body every whit, that it may stand before the throne of grace every whit *clean!*

[15]Then, make thy prayers unto Him, giving glory, power and praise unto Him—and in this manner may that which has *seemed* to be to thee as a hindrance become a steppingstone to the glory of thine own soul!

[16]We are through.

Chapter 9

DEALING WITH CHANGE

READING 1723-1

The signs of change are all about us. The '90s are proving to be a decade of turmoil, unpredictability, and transformation. But lest we think that we are the first ones of the twentieth century to face this challenge, let's remember that other decades—not really so long ago—had to deal with problems every bit as great as our own today. This reading from Edgar Cayce—given in the autumn of 1938—came right in the midst of such a period. What makes it especially noteworthy and relevant for us decades later is its theme: *dealing with change from a spiritual perspective.*

Recall what was going on in 1938. The world was still in the throes of the Depression. In spite of the New Deal programs, history shows that severe economic hardship was the norm in the late '30s. What's more, the signs of almost inevitable war loomed on the horizon. In fact, World War II was to begin just ten months after Cayce gave reading 1723-1.

This spiritual message about dealing with the stresses of change was not delivered to one of the economic or political leaders of the era. Instead, the recipient was a common fellow—a twenty-five-year-old man whose occupation was driving a petroleum tank truck. This was an individual of modest estate in the world of his times. But the universal themes addressed in the advice from Cayce can speak to our contemporary condition, wherever we find ourselves.

Two themes seem particularly powerful in this reading. One is the dynamic tension between the changeless and that which changes. Each of us must confront and wrestle with this paradoxical situation. How do we stay involved with the exhilarating process of transformation *and also* stay connected to that which is changeless and eternal?

The other theme concerns the power given to us by free will—the ability to make changes in our innate disposition and temperament. Here we're talking about the tough but essential work of making daily choices that transform us into the fullness of what we can be.

The opening paragraphs of this reading deal principally with a description of Mr. [1723]'s personality characteristics. Try looking at this part of the reading in the following way. Paragraph 4 has some "bad news." It is pretty blunt and probably wasn't easy for him to accept graciously when he first read the words.

Paragraphs 6 through 14 create another section—this one includes some "good news." These nine paragraphs follow a format Cayce almost always used in a life reading: astrological language to describe a more detailed picture of strengths and weaknesses. Here the young man receives some hopeful advice about using his talents constructively. He's given a vision of what his soul is here to contribute.

The bridge between the two sections—paragraph 4 on the one hand, and paragraphs 6-14, on the other—is the spiritual principle delivered in paragraph 5. The habit patterns that can get in the way of our spiritual progress are only tendencies or "inclinations." Any of us can, in

fact, change. We have free will and that freedom makes
personal change a very real option. We've each had previous experiences with personal change and those
memories stand as proof of what is possible.

What makes all this material about personality habits
and disposition so important is the following psychological principle: In times of change, either our weaknesses or our strengths come to the forefront. The choice
is up to us. Think about what happens in response to
natural catastrophes, economic chaos, or war. For some
people it sparks deeds of extraordinary caliber; in others, it leads to pitiful acts of selfishness.

Or, think about this principle in terms of your own experience. In times of turmoil and unpredictability, isn't it
either your worst faults that seem to get magnified or
your greatest strengths that step forward? It may well be
that the better we know ourselves the more likely it is
that we can use free will to ensure it's our best that comes
out in stressful, challenging times. And, as Cayce points
out, the more clearly we have a potent spiritual ideal, the
more likely it is that changing times will bring out our
best. For Mr. [1723], his reading specifically identifies
kindness (see paragraphs 5 and 17) as the key to his ability to make personal changes in the midst of a world
changing rapidly around him.

The other important theme in Cayce's message is just
as valuable to our own understanding of how to deal
with change. In essence it's this: We must discover the
living reality of the "changeless," even when we're facing
a world that's changing so fast we can't keep up with it.
And how do we connect with this elusive, "changeless"
side of life? The answer is through deeds that are so loving and kind that they create something that lives on and
on. Take a careful look at paragraph 15. That one sen-
tence, and the two paragraphs that follow, are probably
the most eloquent and powerful commentary Cayce

ever gave on dealing with times of change.

What those words say to me is that an inward, meditative retreat each day isn't enough, if I aspire to make a personal connection to the "changeless." If I want to be linked to that which lives on and on, then something more is needed. I have to be good *for something*—that is, for someone who stands in need of a hopeful word or a moment of kind attention. As unpretentious as that may sound, it's the key to dealing with times of change.

THE READING

This psychic reading, 1723-1, was given by Edgar Cayce on November 1, 1938. The conductor was Gertrude Cayce.

[1]GC: You will give the relation of this entity and the universe, and the universal forces; giving the conditions that are as personalities, latent and exhibited in the present life; also the former appearances in the earth plane, giving time, place and the name, and that in each life which built or retarded the development of the entity; giving the abilities of the present entity, and that to which it may attain, and how. You will answer the questions he submits, as I ask them:

[2]EC: Yes, we have the records here of that entity now known as or called [1723].

[3]In giving the interpretation of the records as we find them, these are chosen with the desire and hope to make the experience a helpful one in the entity's application of self in the present toward a mental and spiritual development with reference to the material—which should be the result of such application.

[4]Then, in viewing the records generally—but without respect to what the entity has done or may do regarding the urges which arise—we find the inclination for the entity to oft be called material-minded, hard-hearted,

stubborn, and without any thought of these things which bespeak of affections for affection's sake.

⁵These as given are inclinations. The entity has altered and may alter such inclinations—or they arise as conditions which may be magnified, and thus—though bringing material gains, even at times positions of importance—unless there is the development of the milk of human kindness within the experience it may be, it may become a very lonesome, a very disturbing experience throughout this sojourn.

⁶In the interpreting of the astrological aspects, which are as reference to the interims of experiences, not all experiences are given but rather those which have the greater bearing upon the entity in this present period of activity in this sojourn.

⁷And as first indicated, these are given with the desire that the warnings, the information may be made to be a helpful influence in the entity's application of its dealings with its fellow man.

⁸Jupiter we find as the greater ruling influence. Hence in any endeavor in which the entity's activities are to serve the masses or groups of people, the entity will find a channel through which the greater material and mental as well as spiritual forces may arise.

⁹Hence in those channels where there is the sale of products which are to have their effect or activity among the many—or the gathering of data as a statistician, or records of any nature. All of these become a part of the entity's development, and channels through which the greater influence may come for greater helpful experiences; provided those characteristics as indicated become a part of their application.

¹⁰In Mercury we find with the adverse influence in Venus, with Mars as well as Saturn, there are the influences which become a part of the entity's environs or surroundings.

[11]Hence of high mental abilities is the entity—with the liking for or desire for study—the liking or desire for knowledge. But such knowledge as statistics, such knowledge as of the natures where the influences or activities of individuals or groups are to be maintained, is not to be used wholly for self in self-aggrandizement or self-advantage taken over others.

[12]To be sure, it may be used in such measures as to bring greater material opportunities, greater material successes, but at the behest—and not at the advantage taken over less fortunate ones or those who have not applied themselves.

[13]In Venus we find the necessity for the cultivation of influences wherein not merely ideals or idealistic principles are held, but ideals to be adhered to—in mental, in material, but based upon spiritual attributes. These are to be cultivated. So, the doing and being virtuous for the very *nature* of that impelling influence which it brings into the experience of the entity is necessary for cultivation in the activities.

[14]These in their first applications may bring some disturbing influences, yet to know that obligations are opportunities as well as duties, as well as privileges, is a lesson the entity should learn—and it will make for greater contentment, greater peace and happiness in its experiences as it deals with the changing influences and forces which arise.

[15]Then know that while the life is in a changing world, with changing friendships, changing environs and changes of every nature—unless there is accomplished that which lives on and *on* in the heart and soul, little has been or may be accomplished by self in its dealings with its fellow man.

[16]Be acquainted, then, with that home beyond. Take time not merely to be holy or good, but good for something—good in that ye bring each day some new hope,

some new opportunity, some new experience in the life of someone—a boy, a child, a babe, an old person who has lost the way in one manner or another. Thus ye will gradually build those steps which may carry you beyond the vale of those who see only the material blessings. For ye will know of Whom, in Whom ye have heard that "His words passeth not away."

¹⁷So, though changes come, though the heavens may be in turmoil, though the earth and all the activities may be in riot, thy deeds done in such a way and manner will not change but live in the heart and the mind in such a manner as to bring that peace and harmony which comes only to those who take thought of just being kind to the other fellow!

¹⁸Know that if you would be forgiven, if you would have friends, if you would know peace you must *make* friends, be kind, be joyous, be *content*—but *never* satisfied! For that longing which arises to better thyself is not merely that thy body may take ease, or that ye may gratify the appetites thereof! but it is rather that glory of the hope within for the greater knowledge of the spiritual life to *grow* and *bloom* in thy workaday life.

¹⁹For only that character of spiritual thought that is a practical thing, that may be lived and experienced day by day, is worthy of thy acceptation.

²⁰And it is thy nature—but cultivate it! For this will bring greater opportunities physically, mentally, and open the door of thy consciousness to the unseen forces that make men *not* afraid!

[This is the lengthy opening discourse to his life reading. The remaining information in the reading contains material with personal, rather than universal, applicability.]

Chapter 10

FINDING VOCATION IN A TROUBLED WORLD

READING 333-1

In a chaotic, constantly changing world, how can we find our true calling? How do we sort through the limitations and frustrations to find genuinely meaningful vocation or "right livelihood," as it's called in the Buddha's Eightfold Path? In essence this was the need addressed in every one of Edgar Cayce's so-called "life readings"— clairvoyant pictures of a soul's background and its prospects for growth and service in the present incarnation.

But finding right vocation is an important subject in many other types of Cayce readings—not the life readings alone—as this mental-spiritual advice reading to a forty-nine-year-old man illustrates. In fact, this reading is so inspirational with its message about finding purpose in life that no less a figure among Cayce's supporters than David Kahn wrote: "I've never seen a finer reading."

From the background on Mr. [333], we learn that he was a deeply frustrated sales engineer working in Depression-era New York City. How did Cayce go about offering advice to this mid-life man who was facing crises, both with his family finances (due to inadequate employment) and his seeming failure to have found a meaningful life's work? Cayce's approach began with the suggestion given by his wife Gertrude at the start of the reading. Notice that this suggestion is out of the ordinary, emphasizing how this one man's problem is part of a challenge that is shared with millions of others ("the great masses of common people struggling for they know not what").

What we find in the body of the reading is not a set of straightforward recommendations concerning where to find a better job. Cayce's approach is less aimed at occupation-finding and more directed toward helping Mr. [333] reorient his entire outlook on life. Only by creating the proper frame of mind as a foundation would he have prospects of then resolving the dilemmas of his career and personal finances.

First Cayce addresses the essence of the problem. In paragraph 3 the conditions are described as a test of ideal and of personal free will. This inspirational message seems to be intended to restore this man's belief in his own ideals and to create a context for everything else that follows in the reading. With paragraph 4 Cayce then begins to outline a strategy for how Mr. [333] might proceed with his quest to find meaningful vocation and adequate material supply to support his family. First is the principle to take life one day at a time and to make the best use of his talents in whatever situation he finds himself. Be in the present moment, looking for the workings of God in today's situation.

In that same paragraph is a potent phrase that we might easily overlook: " . . . *preserve* same in thine *own* heart . . . " This is a spiritual discipline from which we can probably all benefit. It means to commit to memory those moments of clear awareness when we see life and ourselves with authentic spiritual vision. We all have these special moments—some of us more often than others. But virtually everyone suffers from a kind of amnesia in which our troubled, fast-paced material lives coax us into forgetting the spiritual truths we've previously glimpsed. To "preserve in our own heart" those special moments of insight and understanding is the discipline of placing them in a type of memory that stays accessible every day.

It's obvious from this reading that one of Mr. [333]'s big concerns was how much he should "take thought to the morrow"—that is, plan ahead for his financial future and anticipate the problems that might arise. In both paragraphs 6 and 8, Cayce suggests that it's OK to look ahead but it should be done in conjunction with keeping the temple of one's physical body and conscious mind purified. The critical ingredient is to maintain a connection with God, who will "converse with thee in the courts of thine own temple." If that line of communication is left open and free, then the guidance and support can flow, even in the midst of making practical common-sense decisions about the "secular things of life," including vocation.

Fear is the great disrupter of this process, as Cayce emphasizes in the middle of paragraph 6. And ultimately, faith is the antidote. Not "confidence," but a deeper and more significant potential of human character we call "faith." The difference here is crucial. Confidence rests upon experiences that relate to the material world; whereas faith depends upon understanding and experience that transcends familiar time and space limits. Faith is knowing firsthand the reality of the spiritual world.

Overall, Cayce's clairvoyant view of this man's prospects was optimistic. In answer to the question about remaining with his present employer (see paragraph 10), the reading appears to offer a hopeful prophecy: "in no uncertain measures" there will come into your life the means to meet your family's needs—but it will come "through other channels" than this present employer. And although it took some time—in this case about eleven months —the prophecy was seemingly fulfilled. Following the advice in this reading as diligently as he could, Mr. [333] found more meaningful and lucrative work. He wrote appreciatively to Mr. Cayce: "This past week has been a busy one for me . . . including a great blessing to me and my family through being able to secure a job better than the one I just left, and including opportunities for development that may mean much . . . Now that is what my friends call a miracle for these times, but know what I do, I regard it as a fulfillment of the promises made to me in that wonderful spiritual message you secured for me last June."

THE READING

This psychic reading, 333-1, was given by Edgar Cayce on June 22, 1932. The conductor was Gertrude Cayce.

[1]GC: You will have before you the body and inquiring mind of [333], who is at . . . N.Y., who seeks consideration, advice and guidance, from the Master and the Creative Forces, in regard to the worldwide economic problem which confronts himself and family, together with the great masses of common people struggling for they know not what. You will answer the questions which he has sincerely, respectfully and faithfully submitted.

[2]EC: We have the body, the enquiring mind, [333]; also those conditions, economic and otherwise, that confront the body.

[3]In this relation, there are ever those elements, as was given of old, confronting each and every individual: "There is today set before thee good and evil, life and death. Choose thou whom ye will serve," and let the answer ever be, "Others may do as they may, but for me

and my house, we will serve the *living* God." Not one that may not listen or harken to the cry of those that are faithful. One that is not unmindful of the fear, the doubt, that stalks abroad in the land at this particular period in the history of the land when greed, avarice, misunderstanding, has taken the judgment away from many and they struggle for that they know not what. Will all come and—even those that fear—but open their minds, their hearts, their souls, to that cry that has ever been to His peoples, "Will ye be my people, I will be your God"—"Are not two sparrows sold for a farthing? Consider the lilies of the field, how they toil not, neither do they spin, or the grass—that today is and tomorrow is cast in the oven." Whether ye live or whether ye die, ye are in the Lord, and let Him have His way with thee, for He does not suffer even the unfaithful to be tempted without preparing a way of escape. If the righteous shall scarcely be saved, where does the ungodly appear?

[4]Then, use those talents thou hast in hand day by day, and there is given that thou hast need of, will ye but turn your heart, your mind, your soul, to seeking how in loving kindness ye may show in some measure that love, that faith, that confidence, that is aroused in thine own breast with the knowledge that He is in *thine* holy temple; for thine body is indeed the temple of the living God, and let the desires then of the eye, the weaknesses of the flesh, the call for those things that so easily beset thyself, keep silent—*wait* ye on the Lord. Not in some great manifestation that would make for tempestuous doubts in the lives of many, but here a little, there a little, ye that are the salt of the earth, *preserve* same in thine *own* heart, that the *Lord* may have *His* way; for He has not willed that *any* should perish, but that *all* may present their bodies a *living* sacrifice, holy, acceptable unto Him, for it is but a reasonable service.

[5]That the cares of this world, the deceitfulness of

place, position, that is sought oft among men, in the owning of houses, lands, and of those things that would wean men's hearts away from following in the straight and narrow path—but know *He* knows what ye have need of before ye ask Him, and wilt thou keep thine heart He will even open the heavens to pour out a blessing upon thee.

[6]In *this* manner, then, should self meet those conditions that seem to confront self at this time. Not that one takes not thought, but by taking thought let it be rather, "Are the courts of my temple a dwelling place of the living God? Or have I rather set up those idols of the earth that are earthy?" And as self *finds* the way clarified by the keeping of the courts and the temple cleansed, "Make not my Father's house a den—" Rather let thy yeas be yea and thy nays be nay, that *He* may come in the heat of the day or the cool of the evening and converse with thee in the courts of thine own temple; for thus doth He speak among men, and thus doth men find that which overcomes fear; for when fear enters, then doth one allow the doors of the temple to be broken up, and there enters in thoughts of the carnal forces that ever war with man, with man's good intent. These kept clean bring the glory of the Father through the Way that the Son has opened for all who seek His face. "The cattle are mine, as the silver and the gold, saith the Lord. These have been prepared that mine children shall not want, even in a *weary* land," but as the rock that casts shadows for those that are athirst, and brings forth its waters that those may be supplied who seek in the shadow of same, so in *this* temple of thine know He will guide, guard and direct in the way that *thou* may become a rock for thine brother; for he that lendeth to the Lord has covered much that may be called amiss by others. *Keep* the way clear.

[7]Ready for questions.

[8](Q) Am I wrong in giving thought to the morrow,

when I should be placing confidence in divine influence, or trust in God?

(A) Use rather the opportunities day by day in such a manner that the *glory* of the Lord may be shown in the strength of the mind, of the body, to meet the emergencies that arise as concerning the secular things of life; for as these offices may appear to become more slack in this or that direction, the greater *faith*—rather than confidence—in His promises makes for *strength* in body and mind to meet those things necessary. Let the *desires* of the physical grow less, as the desires of the spiritual would make thee strong in His might.

[9](Q) Am I among those who shall be blessed by being found so doing when the Lord cometh?

(A) Keep thy face to the light, and the shadows of doubt fall *far* behind. So thou wilt find thy name written among those who loved his fellow man, even as He walked among men—called them His brother—gave of that bounty supplied by the closer communion day by day. "Give us *this* day our *daily* bread. *Forgive,* O Lord, as I forgive my brother." In walking in this light does the strength to do the physical deeds come in the body, even as the strength to bear His own cross, even as the strength to give, "Father, *forgive* them—they know not what they do!" This brought ministering from the Father of light, the Father of power, the Father of love to man, that we are *His* brothers and heirs to the *kingdom* of light through ministering in word, in deed, to our fellow man in His Name; for there be no name named under heaven that brings hope, joy, life, as the *name* of the *Christ* among men!

[10](Q) Am I wrong in remaining in my present employment? [sales engineer for steel and metal products company]

(A) Remain in the employment, that there may come—*with* the building up on every side—that which will enable self, and those the body serves, to *know* even the rocks and hills cry out, "*Blessed* is he who comes in the name of the Lord!"

Does the remuneration in the present surroundings not supply that necessary to meet those payments that may come upon the earthly abode, then those surroundings—as well as the abilities to obtain through other channels those means that will enable you to supply that lacking—will be given thee in no uncertain measures, *will* there be held, "I *am* the Lord's—He *is* my defense—in Him *will* I put my trust—and I *will* be faithful to my brother to the best of my physical and my mental abilities." Not becoming a pest in speaking of those things. "When there is the cry for bread, doth He give them a stone?" Rather give him a portion of that *thou* hast, and together *seek* the Lord!

[11](Q) Are the men who are paying me a wage doing so in full measure of their ability, justice and consideration for my responsibilities?

(A) As ye measure, so shall it be measured to you again! "The Lord *bless* them, the Lord keep them, and make His face to shine upon them, in such measures that *together in* the trials may there come the blessed understanding that all must work together to meet the measures that are being brought to all during this seeking period of those that have wandered far afield," for the Lord *keepeth* those that fear—yea, love and trust in the fear of the Lord!

These are capable of being approached by responsibilities and measures builded upon self. "In the way ye would have them deal with you, deal ye with them!"

[12](Q) Would it be right for me to seek employment during the night hours with a wholesale bakery or gas service station, to help increase my income?

(A) Seek and ye shall find! Keep in the way of the Lord and the way is opened unto thee to meet those needs for thine self and for thine dependent ones, as well as that that may be given or lent to the Lord through aiding thy brother! *Seek*—when needed.

[13]We are through for the present.

Chapter 11

A New Order in World Affairs

READING 3976-18

History moves in cycles. The amount of national and international change that was going on in the late 1930s—when reading 3976-18 was given—and in the early 1940s has been revisited in our own times, over fifty years later. They are swift, unexpected, and dramatic changes that leave us wondering where the world is headed.

Look carefully at this short but powerful statement that Cayce made slightly more than a year before World War II began. Its themes and its message are just as potent today. A "new order of conditions" is arising. If Communism in Eastern Europe can collapse and the Israelis and the PLO can move toward peace, what isn't possible?

The positive potential in these times of change depends on the attitudes and ideals of individual people, according to Cayce. A very specific outlook and ethical code is described in this reading. Being each other's loving guardians or "keepers" is one way it's described. "Leveling" is another. It boils down to simply this: *oneness.* In a world of extraordinary diversity, the human family must find ways to stay in touch with its underlying oneness.

Some of the most insightful and eloquent interpretations of the Cayce World Affairs readings have been made by political science professor Dr. Linda Quest. Two books published by A.R.E. Press more than twenty years ago—*The Politics of Hope* and *Peace by Choice*—present a view of modern history in light of Cayce's vision of spiritual law and social dynamics. Oneness is clearly a centerpiece of that vision. More recently, at ceremonies of Atlantic University, Dr. Quest's graduation address used reading 3976-18 (and other Cayce World Affairs readings) as an inspiration. Her insights and interpretations shed new light on the challenges we collectively face as a new world order emerges. In part, she said:

Since 1989 there has been a "pole shift" in world affairs. There's also been a pole shift in your backyard, in your city streets, and in your hometown. This remarkable transition can best be seen as it plays out in the current events of the world and of nations.

The issue can be seen as the tension between two sides of a paradox. We must have both freedom and the sense of community. How will we achieve it? Graduates of Atlantic University might well take the transpersonal wisdom which they've cultivated in their studies and apply it to their professions, occupations, and careers. But that wisdom must be taken everywhere else, also— to the realm of politics, to the front curbs of our neighborhoods, to the school yards, the laundromats, and every other place where we find ourselves in daily life.

We are at a historic moment—the like of which has never been before in all of human experience. The rise of freedom has brought difficulty. We can see the problem this way: There were 186 sovereign states in the world at the start of 1993, and a number of additional affiliated territories bringing the total number of "places" to 252. The number might seem large, but it isn't when you realize that there are at least 5,000 "nations" in the world! By the word *nations,* I'm referring to entities which have language, culture, history, government, territories, or territorial claims. These 5,000 are somehow squeezed into 252 places.

We can notice that many of these national entities are tribal or ancestral in character. They are not recognizably modern in many, many instances, but the rise in freedom has encouraged them to cut loose. Many are engaged in acts of succession, and some are engaged in a movement for annexation. The people involved may call their efforts the struggle for freedom, but not *all of those who are struggling for freedom are also struggling toward the twenty-first century.* Some, whether they know it or not, are beating a path toward extinction. Those who insist upon the schisms, the divisions, and the separations, block themselves, and they heave stumbling blocks in the path of others as well. This is the road of the reckoning and what Cayce called "leveling." What will come out in the end for these people is probably the loss of their language, culture, history, government, and property, *if any of those elements is used in opposition to the principle of one humanity or the value of the individual.* Those entities—those "nations"—can't endure.

In attempting to make sense of the modern world situation, the Edgar Cayce material is extremely useful. The criteria in the Edgar Cayce readings for telling the difference between the path to freedom and the path to extinction are simply two:

The first is *oneness.* One life, one force, one source, reflected in the oneness of all humanity and in the value of each individual as the universe in miniature. Repeatedly Edgar Cayce warned against setting anything—any division, any schism higher than the Fatherhood of God and the brotherhood of man. Cayce said that these divisions would become as "naught." They would become as nothing compared with the oneness.

The second criterion is *choice.* Choice was specified in the Edgar Cayce readings as the controlling factor in the way in which human beings claim their birthright: free will.

So, as the Cayce readings and Dr. Quest emphasize, the choice is ours, even in our seemingly little deeds and passing thoughts. What kind of new world order are we helping to create?

THE READING

This psychic reading, 3976-18, was given by Edgar Cayce on June 20, 1938. The conductor was Gertrude Cayce.

[1]GC: You will have before you the work of the Association for Research and Enlightenment, Inc., in studying and presenting the psychic work of Edgar Cayce. It is desired to present on Monday evening, June 27th, material presented through this channel, for the Seventh Annual Congress, on national and international affairs which will be in keeping with the ideal and purposes of the work being undertaken by the Association. You will consider the type of audience which will be present, the need for informative information which will not be spectacular or sensational, yet that will be constructive. Advise us also as to the manner of presentation. You will give the first discourse on this subject.

[2]EC: Yes, we have the work of the Association for Research and Enlightenment, Inc., and the policies and ideals and purposes of same; as related to national and international affairs that would not be spectacular but constructive—and in keeping with the ideals.

[3]As has been and is being understood by many, there are changes being wrought in the nation, as well as in the interrelationships with other nations.

[4]All of these may be considered from the one angle.

[5]It is also understood, comprehended by some, that a new order of conditions is to arise; that there must be many a purging in high places as well as low; that there must be the greater consideration of each individual, each soul being his brother's keeper.

[6]There will then come about those circumstances in the political, the economic and the whole relationships where there will be a leveling—or a greater comprehension of this need.

[7]For as the time or the period draws near for these changes that come with the new order, it behooves all of those who have an ideal—as individuals, as well as groups or societies or organizations, to be practicing, applying same in their experience—and their relationships as one to another.

[8]For unless these are up and doing, then there must indeed be a new order in *their* relationships and their activities.

[9]For His ways will carry through. For as He gave, "Though the heavens and the earth may pass away, my word will *not* pass away."

[10]All too often has this message been forgotten in the pulpits and in the organizations, not only in the national relationships but in the international relationships.

[11]And as the dealings are as one to another, unless these are in keeping with those tenets they must fail; for all power in heaven and in earth hath been given into His hands.

[12]Then as we approach all phases of human relationships, these must be taken into consideration.

[13]And there *cannot* be one measuring stick for the laborer in the field and the man behind the counter, and another for the man behind the money-changers. *All* are equal—not only under the material law but under the *spiritual*.

[14]And *His* laws, *His* will, will not come to naught!

[15]Though there may come those periods when there will be great stress, as brother rises against brother, as group or sect or race rises against race—yet the leveling must come.

[16]And *only* those who have set their ideal in Him and practiced it in their dealings with their fellow man may expect to survive the wrath of the Lord.

[17]In thy dealings, then—whether at home, in thy dealings with state or the national situations, or the international affairs—there must come *all* under that purpose, that desire.

[18]And then there should be, there *will* be those rising to power that are able to meet the needs. For none are in power but that have been given the opportunity by the will of the Father—from which all power emanates.

[19]Hence those will be leveled with the purpose, "My word shall *not* fail!"

[20]In presenting such—well that it be given as extract, or as that from such sources to be used or taken as those present see fit.

[21]We are through for the present.

Chapter 12

Preparing for the Coming of Christ

READING 587-6

More often than not, for those of us who are of the Christian faith in this busy, consumer-oriented society, the Christmas holiday means making gift lists and scheduling travel time to see relatives. So we often need reminders that there's something much more meaningful about Christmas. If you celebrate this holiday, Cayce reading 587-6 can be such a reminder.

This eloquent reading was given for a forty-five-year-old Protestant homemaker. She had received a life reading a year earlier, and in this follow-up reading she asks for more facts about a lifetime in Palestine two thousand years ago. Cayce's details about this period—especially the preparations for the birth of Jesus—give an inspiring message about Christmas and the coming of Christ directly into human affairs.

If there is a central theme in this reading, it's *preparation*. Jesus' birth was not merely a lucky event for humanity or simply a graceful deed of the Creator. According to Cayce, Jesus' birth was possible because God's love was able to manifest *through* a group of people who had consciously and diligently prepared themselves for just this possibility. These people were the Essenes, a mysterious group known to biblical scholars and historians.

The Essenes understood that this was a season of great possibility and selected a handful of girls as candidates. One might become the mother through whom Christ would come. According to Cayce's clairvoyant vision, this very soul that was now Mrs. [587] had been one of the selected candidates and underwent many years of dedicated consecration—physically, mentally, and spiritually. And although it was Mary who was chosen, the soul that was now Mrs. [587] had stayed close to the people and events of Jesus' life.

Reading 587-6 has many intriguing images of these familiar events—for example, the Wise Men and the shepherds in the field. But equally important to our understanding of Christmas are Cayce's reminders of what the Christ came to bring us. Paragraph 6 describes what Jesus-who-became-the-Christ taught humanity: The truth is written within the hearts of each one of us. It's not in a book or a building. The true spirit of Christmas is found *within* our consciousness. That's a teaching we can really apply in the hectic, demanding holiday season when there are so many outer pressures.

In paragraph 16 the theme of *change* is emphasized. By His coming into the world, something was profoundly altered. Cayce describes it poetically—the course of the stars in their movement around the earth was changed. What's this all about? Surely it's not just astronomical conditions.

The movement is within the human soul. Something was awakened in the soul-mind of *every* individual, whether or not they were physically incarnated then. A quickening hope was unleashed within the human psyche. A new sense of real possibility was stimulated. And that is exactly what Christmas is still all about!

How do we prepare *this year* to experience its meaning more deeply? This reading gives hints.

Consider the idea of dedication and consecration. It's probably not realistic to ask of ourselves the demanding purification lifestyle of the Essenes. But we *can* ask ourselves, In what small-scale way am I ready to rededicate myself? Maybe a positive emotion you'll express more often—joy, hopefulness, or appreciation. Maybe a spiritual discipline you'll try a little harder to practice daily, such as meditation or dream study. Or, perhaps it will be a commitment to reach out regularly to others in a creative way.

In fact, the meaning of Christmas and of Christ's life is deeply rooted in such a social sphere. It's in *relationships* that we connect with the Christ living within us all. Paragraph 16 reminds us of the biblical principle that "As ye do it unto the least of my brethren ye do it unto me." A good way to practice that sort of rededication during the Christmas season is to live the challenging words of this reading: to express "the kind words spoken to those that are in doubt and in fear." That simple discipline is a powerful way to reconsecrate ourselves, to participate in an *ongoing preparation* for the full manifestation of the universal Christ Consciousness—a preparation that is timeless.

THE READING

This psychic reading, 587-6, was given by Edgar Cayce on October 18, 1935. The conductor was Hugh Lynn Cayce.

[1]HLC: You will have before you the soul-entity of [587], born December 11, 1890, in Chicago, Illinois, present in this room. You will give a complete history of the entity's appearance in the earth plane as Edithia at the period of the Master's entrance into the earth plane. Particular stress is desired on the urges and influences of this expe-

rience on the present life. You will answer the questions that may be asked.

[2]EC: Yes, we have the soul-entity here, and the period of manifestations in the earth during the period of the Master's entrance.

[3]In giving the interpretation of that as we find as a record in the experience of this soul-entity, it is well for the moment that there be given some conception of the conditions that surrounded that particular portion of the earth's spheres and activity of the period; also as a background, as it were, for this entity, this soul's experience as Edithia, in that particular phase of its development.

[4]We find, then, the entity was of the household of those that had been a portion of the lineage where there had been set aside the men of the household for a definite service in the activities of the peoples of the day. Not merely in the thought of that termed in the present as the people of Israel, but rather that as understood by those peoples of the day—the greater meaning of the word Israel—those called of God for a service before the fellow man.

[5]Then, that group, those of the particular sect to which the household of Edithia belonged, had—through study, through experience, through longing and desires—been among those that had been prepared. And there had come those periods when there were to be the changes in the order of things. Man as man had been looked upon as the only correct line of understanding or application, and woman (or women) as an individual was only to obey the master of the house. There had been, then, the understanding of that which had been promised from the beginning of man's interpretation of his relationships to a Creative Force or God, a *correct* interpretation of "and the seed of the woman shall bruise his head."

[6]There was then the choosing of those from the varied activities of that brotherhood, for those that might be chosen of the Lord for the channel through which there might come that beloved Son, who would make the paths straight, who would bring then *man out* of darkness into light; with the understanding that there must be—and would be, through the very expression of that Being in the earth—the understanding that the law was written in the hearts of men, rather than upon tables of stone; that the temple, that the holy of holies was to be within. Also that which had been given as the pattern to those that had made for the calling as of the voice of one in the wilderness for the people that were scattered as a flock without a shepherd. And behold the day, the hour, the time had come when that shepherd must lead forth His flock, His brethren again into the light of the countenance of an All-Merciful Father.

[7]This entity then, Edithia, was among the daughters that were chosen as those that were to dedicate, consecrate their bodies, their minds, their service to become a channel. And with others was chosen in the earlier period of its earthly activity.

[8]Hence in that environ, in that atmosphere of expectancy, in that atmosphere of promise was the directing of the entity's thought, the entity's activity made during those experiences.

[9]And when there was chosen that one to whom there had come that as a gift from on High, the entity *knew* then Mary, Martha, those of the household of Cleopas, those of the household of Anna, of Joseph, and those of the brotherhood of that order called the Essenes in that particular land.

[10]There were those periods through which the entity as one chosen or called among those for the dedicating of their activities, experienced not only those periods when the law demanded that the children, the sons were

to be destroyed, but that even those who were consecrated might be abused the more by those activities of
Roman power, or the authority that had been given
among that brotherhood as that *from* which man was to
be cleansed.

[11]In that environ, then, with those conditions that
arose about the entity, did the early years, the early experiences come to this entity.

[12]During those years of preparation of the Master in
the various fields of activity, again there were the years
of longing, the periods of oppression, the periods of fear
and doubt, the periods of the attempt to be disbanded
by those more and more in authority.

[13]Hence when there was proclaimed of the son of
Elizabeth that he had through the prayers, the activities
of those consecrated souls, become one capable in the
flesh of renouncing the priesthood and to become as an
outcast that there might be made known what had been
promised by those of old, that he should be as the voice
of the one crying in the wilderness, "Prepare ye the way,
for the day of the Lord *is* at hand," the entity was among
those that aided in those preparations. And it was a fol-
lower of same, owing to those periods of the preparation
and the depressing periods when there had been the
persecutions of those that scattered those chosen for
those offices.

[14]Then, in applying these to the urges that appear in
the present experience, is there little wonder that the
doubts and fears from those in authority should not
make those recurrent activities in the very soul of the
entity; that unless there arises some one who would defy
custom, one that would defy authority, one that would
defy in a manner even that which has become as the
natural experience of those to keep harmonious experiences? For the day will arise, even as it arose with the
entity then, when he that separates himself becomes

rather the one that declares to all.

[15]And the entity has found self oft contemplating the face of the Master, on that day when John declared, "Behold the lamb of God that taketh away the reproach of his people!"

[16]This brings to the entity that awakening in the present; and more and more the entity should hold to those experiences that arise from those that walked and talked with Him as a man, *as* those that would become ones with that activity that *changed*—as it were—the course of the stars in their movement about the earth, and that becomes in the hearts and souls of men that hope which *quickens* as the water of life, that heals as does the touch of His hand upon the brow, that awakens as does the kind word spoken to those that are in doubt and in fear. For this is His teaching, "As ye do it unto the least of my brethren ye do it unto me."

[17]The entity from those experiences in the periods of waiting, as many, doubted; yet in the presence of Him—as He increased, and as many of the disciples of John became doubtful when Herod putting forth his hand slew him that there might be the appeasing of a selfish desire because he had spoken against that which answered to the aggrandizing of a fleshly lust—there came the days when Edithia was with those great crowds that cried, "Hosanna! Ye come in the name of the Lord!"

[18]And though they turned into troublesome days, when He—too—was taken from His loved ones, Edithia remained with the holy women that in the period acted for the family as the mourners for Mary, who had been the companion of Edithia in the dedication of self, of self's abilities, of self's body, for those services.

[19]Those experiences become in the present, then, as lights, as halos about the deeds done in the body to show forth His love to *His* brethren till it be fulfilled and He comes again.

[20]Ready for questions.

[21](Q) When and where in Palestine was Jesus born?

(A) In Bethlehem of Judea, in that grotto not marked in the present but called a stable; rather in the den where shelter was had did the *entity* to be sure, look upon the child Jesus.

[22](Q) When was He born?

(A) On the 19th day of what would now be termed March.

[23](Q) And the year?

(A) Dependent upon from what calendar or from what period ye would judge. From the Julian calendar, the year 4. From the Hebrew or the Mosaic calendar, the year 1899.

[24](Q) What was my association with the Wise Men that came seeking the child, and what influence does that have on me now?

(A) As indicated. The entity was among those first chosen to be presented before the Lord as *possible* choices or channels through which those great blessings were to come. So, when the birth came, the *natural* associations were such that the entity was drawn to and about those activities of the parents. And when the Wise Men of the East, or from India, Egypt, the Gobi, came to Jerusalem where there had been the gathering of those that had been of that consecrated group, the *entity* went *with* the Wise Men. For it *awakened within* the entity then that there had been the fulfillment, the completion of that which had been impressed upon the entity in the years of its preparation.

Hence in the present these become, as it were, the words that make for changes in the thought and the activity of the entity *towards* those experiences as with that Son.

[25](Q) What were my experiences with the shepherds who came seeking the Master, and describe my under-

standing of their experience at that time.

(A) As indicated by the records, and as seen here, the shepherds came from the very fact that all nature, all the heavenly hosts, proclaimed that glorious period for man. And as the entity came with the Wise Men to do honor, to give of their substance, the entity—realizing within self that self, in body, in mind, had been dedicated to that service to man, that self might be a channel of blessing—found an awakening in the praise of that given by those shepherds who had *experienced* that cry of the heavenly hosts, "Behold a son is given, and his name is wonderful, counselor!" This awoke within the entity that as may be found in the present, how all nature—the face in the water, the dew upon the grass, the tint and the beauty of the rose, the song of the stars, the mourn of the wind, all proclaim—*now*—the mighty words of a merciful, a loving God.

[26](Q) Give the names of the Wise Men.

(A) This has been given.

[27](Q) What relation did the experience had by Edgar Cayce, of seeing a mentor at the period of my last reading, have with my development. Give name if possible.

(A) Here we have a most holy experience. Keep inviolate, my child, those things that must shortly come to thee, if ye will but harken to the voices within. This *again* is indeed him that *proclaimed* that the day of the Lord *is* at hand—John.

It is indicated in the very manner of his garb; as of one clothed and his raiment shall be white as snow, and they whose sins have been as crimson shall be washed and as wool.

His feet are not of clay; his feet are not as brass, but as of gold—that bespeaks of the endearing messages that may be brought to thee and thine, that thou may indeed *now, fulfill* that for which *then* thou didst dedicate thy life; that ye through thine efforts in flesh may proclaim the wondrous year of the Lord for men!

[28](Q) What relation of John to the White Brotherhood?

(A) As then, the leader; now among the head of the Brotherhood.

[29](Q) What is the meaning of the phenomenon of the spinning sphere which happened to me this morning?

(A) That the awareness within has come of the *nearness* of that as proclaimed from the beginning, "*Know* the Lord thy God is One!" And, who is His mother, His brother, His sister? They that do the will of the Father.

What is the will? The law, the love, as expressed in those words that the Master gave, "Love the Lord thy God with all thine heart, thine body, thy soul; thy brother as thyself."

[30]We are through for the present.

PART FOUR:
BALANCED SPIRITUAL LIVING

Chapter 13

A PATTERN FOR LIVING

READING 1747-5

Each of us is a richly complex individual, a soul with unique characteristics. No one else's joys or problems are exactly like our own. Yet in spite of our differences, something deeper makes us the same. We're all in this game called "material life" together; we're on a common journey with a universal roadmap.

This reading, given for a thirty-seven-year-old factory worker during World War II, beautifully describes a pattern for living that can help anyone meet the challenges of life. As Cayce tells, we all have problems. It's simply part of the human condition. When there are disputes, disappointments, or times of sickness, the real challenge is how we respond. This reading is an outline for the kind of response that brings soul growth and, ultimately, the resolution and healing of our problems.

Cayce's opening statements set the tone for this message. An individual's beliefs and attitudes are the starting point. The most valuable advice is that which helps a person form a basis for viewing life itself. It's counterproductive to focus on the problem prematurely—that is, without an accurate understanding of the big picture. To get such a solid spiritual basis, some "sorting out" is required. A person must be willing and able to discern where various beliefs and assumptions lead. One has to "determine or choose within self that as may be adhered to." One has to make some decisions about core values and convictions.

It's easy to imagine Edgar Cayce giving any one of us this particular reading. His words suggest a way to get the big picture, the overall spiritual context of our lives on the earth. Then he goes into more specific detail about the optimal pattern for meeting any difficulty or challenge. This universal roadmap, this guide for living, has these five essential elements:

1. *Set ideals.* Very carefully select the values, priorities, and motives by which you want to chart your life's path. Be careful not to drift off into pie-in-the-sky wishes. Avoid becoming "merely idealistic," and instead choose ideals that offer some prospect of success. Make your ideals practical—something you can sink your teeth into and concretely work with. They should point toward "working, practical, everyday experiences."

2. *Apply what you believe.* Act on your own values. Even though a solid mental and spiritual foundation is the basis of the pattern, it's not enough. If you stay in the mental realm exclusively, the resolution of your difficulty is unlikely to occur. Admittedly, the mind is the creative faculty that instigates change, but unless you literally *do* what's required of you, how can any condition be healed? " . . . for the holding of a problem does not change it one whit—it is what one does about it that makes the change!"

Furthermore, the very meaning of "sin" points to the absence of action. This is certainly a loaded theological term, but Cayce gives it a new twist: ultimately our spiritual progress is evaluated simply on how well we act on what we know.

3. *Patience is the key.* It is not only the centerpiece to

Cayce's metaphysical description of life, it's also the essential character quality that needs to be developed.

In Cayce's scheme of our orderly universe, humans live in a three-dimensional state of consciousness. Time and space are two of those fundamental measurements. The third, patience, completes the triune by allowing us to meet effectively the demands, paradoxes, and limitations imposed by time and space.

The trick is to comprehend exactly what patience-as-a-dimension-of-living really means. We encounter the word "patience" with our own preconceptions and misunderstanding. But this reading cautions us: "Patience, here, may be the answer—if there is the correct concept of what the proper interpretation of patience is . . . "

For Cayce, patience is considerably more than putting up with delays or tolerantly coping with obnoxious behavior. Instead, patience is more a matter of *seeing clearly,* of viewing life so as to recognize the spiritual reality penetrating physical events. Patience allows us *to understand the purposefulness* behind what's going on in time and space. When misguided people with materialistic views try to influence us, they keep us from this clear vision of purposefulness—they create "the pit that separateth the soul from that patience . . . "

4. *Accept responsibilities to each other.* The optimal pattern for meeting any problem has a social dimension. The key here is responsibility "to" rather than "for." No one can change someone else. No soul is expected to bear the blame for another's error. However, each of us has a task in relationship to others: to see in every person the qualities that we worship in our Maker. Unless we take on that effort, we have "not begun to have the proper concept of universal consciousness."

And what's more, this social dimension has another feature. Because we are examples to those around us, people notice what we say and do—especially how we react to problems. The imitative tendencies of human beings can be used to great advantage in this case because we can inspire and lift others by our own example. "So live that thy friend, thy foe, thy neighbor, may also— through patterning his expressions after thee—find the way . . . "

5. *Expect a responsive God.* Cayce reminds us of "the greater promise from the foundation of the world": God hears our requests for help when times are difficult, and a response is speedily forthcoming. We should expect it and count on it.

Finally, Cayce's advice over fifty years ago to this factory worker assured her of the results that will come by following this optimal pattern. To live according to these five points—especially when life is discouraging or troubling—awakens in us "that peace which each soul seeks, and brings with same healing . . . " Our modern world, over half a century after this reading was given, has its own turmoil and stresses. But the pattern for living—the universal roadmap for meeting problems—equips us to find the peace and healing we all seek.

THE READING

This psychic reading, 1747-5, was given by Edgar Cayce on June 20, 1942. The conductor was Gertrude Cayce.

[1]GC: You will have before you the entity, [1747] . . . Ohio, who seeks a mental and spiritual reading, with information, advice and guidance that will clear the field for her regarding her stand on many things. You will give the entity that needed at this time, answering any questions that may be asked:

[2]EC: Yes, we have the body, the inquiring mind, [1747].

[3]In giving for this entity a mental and spiritual interpretation of the problems as disturb the body in the

present, many phases of those held as tenets or beliefs should be touched upon. But first we would give for the entity that which is the basis for this entity approaching the study of phenomena of every nature that has been and is a part of the experience in the present.

[4]And from same there may be determined that which is not merely idealistic but that as may be a practical, ideal manner of application of the physical relationships with individuals of various degrees of development—of those mental attitudes which should be held in the study of the entity, in the interpreting for individuals of those problems and disturbances which arise in their experience.

[5]Also there may be understood the spiritual and the ideal manner in which the entity may determine or choose within self that as may be adhered to, that as may be questioned, and that as may be discarded in the experience of the entity.

[6]First—there is the consciousness to the body of there being a physical body, a mental body, and the hope or desire for and the knowledge of a spiritual body. These are one—just as the entity finds in the material plane, or the earth-consciousness, that it is of three-dimensional natures. Also, in the analysis of the various studies and approaches to the mental as well as spiritual understanding, the entity finds that there are three phases of man's relationship or man's comprehension. Hence in the earth there is, in reason, only the three-dimensional attitude. Yet there are the experiences of the entity, as well as of others, of more than three-dimensional concepts.

[7]In the Godhead there is found still the three-dimensional concept—God the Father, God the Son, and God the Holy Spirit.

[8]Hence—if this is acceptable to the entity in its conception of that which has been, which is, which may

be—these are still founded in that summed up in "The Lord thy God is One."

[9]Also, in the interpretation of the universe, we find that time and space are concepts of the mental mind, as to an interpretation of or a study into the relationships with man and to the universal or God-consciousness.

[10]Then, there must be another phase in human experience that man also may complete this triune in his study of the mental, the spiritual and the material relationships in this material world.

[11]Patience, here, may be the answer—if there is the correct concept of what the proper interpretation of patience is in the experience of this entity.

[12]Hence these being chosen, they are—then—the basis upon which the reason, the expectation, the application, shall be in dealing with all phases of the experience of the entity in this material relationship.

[13]As is understood, then—Father-God is as the body, or the whole. Mind is as the Christ, which is the way. The Holy Spirit is as the soul, or—in material interpretation—purposes, hopes, desires.

[14]Then, each phase of these has its part to play, its part of influence upon the individual in its relationships to problems, to individuals, to its hopes and fears. For, each has its phase of expression in the activities of the entity.

[15]Hence, as we find, these are then not merely ideals, but they are working, practical, everyday experiences.

[16]Then, as the individual entity meets various problems—with this analysis of the problem—there is the questioning within self as to whether it is purely mental, purely the physical seeking expression, or the desire of the body-fears, the body-temptations, the body's glory, merely the body's satisfaction, or as to whether the problems are purely of the mental. The mind is the builder, for the holding of a problem does not change it one whit—it is what one does about it that makes the change!

[17]Then, to know to do good and not to do it is sin. To know the truth and not give expression is faultfinding in self. Yet know, until an individual entity—in time or space, or in acquaintanceship or in the friendship of an individual—sees in every other entity that he would worship in his Maker, he has not begun to have the proper concept of universal consciousness.

[18]For, the very fact of an individual having a physical consciousness, no matter his state or status in the material plane, is an indication of the awareness that God is mindful of that soul, by giving it an opportunity to express in the material plane.

[19]And thou art thy brother's keeper. Not that ye should impose or impel another entity by thine own ideas, any more than God impels thee. For, He hath given thee the free will, the birthright; which is as the mind, that makes for the alterations. Hence ye may give expression even as He did, who came into the earth that we through Him might have eternal life.

[20]Then, what is thy attitude?

[21]So live that thy friend, thy foe, thy neighbor, may also—through patterning his expressions after thee—find the way to that mercy which is manifested in Him, who gave "I stand at the door and knock—by thy biddings I will enter—by thy rejection I will leave—I hold no grudge."

[22]This requires that expression then, in time and space, of that patience of which He spoke, "In patience become ye aware of your souls."

[23]This, then, is the attitude that ye shall assume. Give that as is asked of thee in the interpreting of the problems; no more, no less. But ever be ready, as He, to enter, to help, to give when asked, when sought. For, as He hath given, which is the greater promise from the foundation of the world, "If ye call, I will hear, and answer speedily—though ye be far away, I will hear—I will answer."

²⁴That is the attitude that the self shall hold towards those problems where there are disputes, discouragings, disappointments. Yea, they oft arise in the experience of all. But think, O Child, how oft thou must have disappointed thy Maker, when He hath given thee the opportunity and calls, "The day of the Lord is at hand," to all of those who will hear His voice.

²⁵Put ye on, then, the whole armor of God, the breastplate of righteousness, the sword of the spirit of truth. *Know* in *whom* ye have believed, as well as in what ye believe. *Live* each day in such a manner as to indicate to everyone ye meet that thou hast an answer for the faith that prompts thee to act in this or that manner.

²⁶Be not discouraged because the way seems hard at times. Know that He heareth thee. For as He hath given, "If ye will keep my law—" And what is His law? It is to love the Lord, to eschew evil—which is the whole duty of man—love thy neighbor as thyself.

²⁷This brings into the consciousness that peace which each soul seeks, and brings with same healing—not only of body but of mind, and keeps the attunement with the spirit of truth.

²⁸Know, too, that His spirit—God's spirit, the Father in the Christ, through the Holy Spirit—beareth witness with thy spirit. And though there comes periods when there are the temptations from all manners of sources, *hear not* those that deny that He hath come in the flesh. Listen to those that bespeak of the cross as the way. Harken not in any manner to those who deny the cross or the cup of bitterness in death.

²⁹These be the channels, these be the ways that the blind leading the blind, both fall into the pit that separateth the soul from that patience, that of Abraham's bosom. "By faith are ye healed, not of thyself—it is the gift of God."

³⁰Let love be abroad, in thy mind, in thy understand-

ing. For the Lord hath looked on thee and loved thee, and hath shown thee the way. Harken to His voice, "Be not afraid—it is I that would speak to thee and thy heart."

[31]Love the Lord. Love His ways. Be patient, be understanding, and He will bring it to pass in thy consciousness of His walking and talking with thee.

[32]Ready for questions.

[33]Let thy prayer oft be:

[34]*Lord, I am Thine. Use me as Thou seest fit—that I may be the greater channel of blessings to those that Thou would, through my effort, bring to Thy understanding. I seek only in the name of the Christ.*

[35]We are through.

Chapter 14

EAST-WEST MEDITATION

READING 2475-1

East meets West. The synthesis of Eastern and Western religious ideas in our own times is of momentous significance. In fact, the famous British historian Arnold Toynbee is reported to have singled out this fusion of spiritual thought. He speculated that hundreds of years from now, as historians look back at the twentieth century, one occurrence will stand out as having been most meaningful: the meeting of Buddhist philosophy with the teachings of the Judeo-Christian tradition.

The Cayce readings have made a valuable contribution in this arena. For many Westerners, this material has been an introduction to concepts and practices more familiar in the East—reincarnation and meditation, especially.

One of the best examples of Cayce as synthesizer of East and West is this remarkable reading on meditation. It was given for a research scientist in his mid-forties—a Quaker who no doubt already had a deep personal interest in contemplation and the inner life. He was particularly curious about the proper use of yoga breathing exercises as a part of his meditation discipline. In response, Cayce gave what is probably his most comprehensive statement of the meaning of meditation and the proper place of techniques such as attention to the breath.

The reading initially establishes the fact that Mr. [2475]'s essential question has merit: The breath *is* of great significance to meditation. (And then later: " . . . the breath is power in itself . . . "—paragraph 34.) However, without an adequate understanding of what is going on in meditation, these special techniques could become detrimental. In paragraph 7, Mr. [2475] is encouraged to study what Cayce had already given on the topic, probably meaning Prayer Group readings 281-13 and 281-41, plus the first chapter, "Meditation," in *A Search for God, Book I.*

After providing in paragraphs 8 through 13 an outline of our threefold nature, Cayce presents in paragraph 14 his principle about breath and meditation—by consciously directing one's breathing, it is possible to awaken an awareness of the oneness of body, mind, and spirit. Our ties to physical consciousness become "looser," and a more universal point of view comes into play.

The impact is through the seven spiritual centers, with the second center—the one Cayce links to the "cells of Leydig" endocrine center—playing a leading role. The expressive, creative side of the soul is allowed to expand by these breathing exercises.

But once one moves in meditation to a more expansive and universal state of awareness, there is a certain vulnerability that is present, too. Cayce's warning is reminiscent of the caution written by Evelyn Underhill in her classic book *Mysticism* (1909). She alerted her readers to "the danger zone of introversion (i.e., meditation)" which comes in the Quiet. Too easily the meditator may settle for something far less than what is possible after having achieved initial progress.

In Cayce's warning, the problem is allowing oneself to be influenced, even "controlled," by factors that don't measure up to a high ideal—the universal Christ. The meditator needs to be careful about stimulating expanded consciousness through breathing techniques if there is no central value, motivation, or ideal directing the process. It's not wise to approach such consciousness-altering methods with one's mind "in neutral." Nor is it a good idea to explore altered consciousness out of curiosity alone—that is, without a *purposeful intent,* as alluded to later in paragraph 34.

Exactly what *are* those influences that can be so detrimental? They're not so much mischievous discarnate entities or impersonal forces of evil. Instead, it's something that we can interpret more internally—something residing in our own unconscious. In paragraph 30 the detrimental forces are referred to as "those influences which constantly seek expressions of self . . . " Later, in answer to the first question, accentuated personal desires are mentioned.

To summarize: As we move meditatively into a more expansive state of awareness, vulnerability to the forces of selfishness becomes a real challenge. This, in part, is what Underhill seemed to warn about, also. The expansive, regenerative, invigorating state of the Quiet can ultimately lead the meditator astray *if* he or she fails to surrender willingly to Something bigger than self.

And so, how can the ideas in this reading be used *in our own meditation practice?* How can we take the prayer- or affirmation-based approach to meditation that's familiar to most A.R.E. members, and combine it with breath-attention exercises which are at the heart of Eastern methods, such as the Buddhist? Cayce's answer to the final question in reading 2475-1 seems highly encouraging, but exactly how does one do it?

One answer might be as follows: Get very clear about

your spiritual ideal. Select a prayerlike affirmation that succinctly gives words to that ideal. Then, use those words as a focal point in every meditation for the first five or ten minutes—completely infusing your mind with the spirit and meaning of those words.

Then, turn your attention to the quiet contemplation of breathing for several minutes. This is the most essential technique of Buddhist meditation.

Avoid any logical analysis or intellectual reasoning about your breath. Just observe it, one breath at a time. *Trust* that "beneath the surface" your ideal is currently transforming and healing you. No conscious effort is now required on your part. After several minutes of such attention to the breath, you may feel moved to return to your affirmation for a while—after which you can go back to the breath.

In this simple way, we can experience the synthesis of Eastern and Western spirituality that many people have found at the heart of Cayce's philosophy.

THE READING

This psychic reading, 2475-1, was given by Edgar Cayce on March 27, 1941. The conductor was Hugh Lynn Cayce.

[1]HLC: You will have before you the body and enquiring mind of [2475] . . . Penna., in special reference to the yoga exercises with which he has been experimenting, in breathing. You will indicate just what has taken place in the body and what should be done from this point, considering the best physical, mental and spiritual development of the entity. You will answer the questions, as I ask them:

[2]EC: Yes, we have the body, the enquiring mind, [2475]; and those conditions, those experiences of the body in the use of yoga exercise in breathing.

[3]To give that as would be helpful to the body at this time, there might be indicated for the body something of that which takes place when such exercises are used—and the experiences had by one so doing.

[4]These exercises are excellent, yet it is necessary that special preparation be made—or that a perfect understanding be had by the body as to what takes place when such exercises are used.

[5]For, *breath* is the basis of the living organism's activity. Thus, such exercises may be beneficial or detrimental in their effect upon a body.

[6]Hence it is necessary that an understanding be had as to how, as to when, or in what manner such may be used.

[7]It would be very well for the body to study very carefully the information which we have given through these sources as respecting meditation. Then this information as may be given here may prove of beneficial effect in the experience of the body.

[8]Each soul, individual or entity, finds these facts existent:

[9]There is the body-physical—with all its attributes for the functioning of the body in a three-dimensional or a manifested earth plane.

[10]Also there is the body-mental—which is that directing influence of the physical, the mental and the spiritual emotions and manifestations of the body; or the way, the manner in which conduct is related to self, to individuals, as well as to things, conditions and circumstances. While the mind may not be seen by the physical senses, it can be sensed by others; that is, others may sense the conclusions that have been drawn by the body-mind of an individual, by the manner in which such an individual conducts himself in relationship to things, conditions or people.

[11]Then there is the body-spiritual, or soul-body—that

eternal something that is invisible. It is only visible to that consciousness in which the individual entity in patience becomes aware of its relationship to the mental and the physical being.

[12]All of these then are one—in an entity; just as it is considered, realized or acknowledged that the body, mind and soul are one—that God, the Son and the Holy Spirit are one.

[13]Then in the physical body there *are* those influences, then, through which each of these phases of an entity may or does become an active influence.

[14]There may be brought about an awareness of this by the exercising of the mind, through the manner of directing the breathing.

[15]For, in the body there is that center in which the soul is expressive, creative in its nature—the Leydig center.

[16]By this breathing, this may be made to expand—as it moves along the path that is taken in its first inception, at conception, and opens the seven centers of the body that radiate or are active upon the organisms of the body.

[17]This in its direction may be held or made to be a helpful influence for specific conditions, at times—by those who have taught, or who through experience have found as it were the key, or that which one may do and yet must not do; owing to whatever preparation has been made or may be made by the body for the use of this ability, this expression through the body-forces.

[18]As this life-force is expanded, it moves first from the Leydig center through the adrenals, in what may be termed an upward trend, to the pineal and to the centers in control of the emotions—or reflexes through the nerve forces of the body.

[19]Thus an entity puts itself, through such an activity, into association or in conjunction with all it has *ever* been or may be. For, it loosens the physical consciousness to the universal consciousness.

[20]To allow self in a universal state to be controlled, or to be dominated, may become harmful.

[21]But to know, to feel, to comprehend as to *who* or as to *what* is the directing influence when the self-consciousness has been released and the real ego allowed to rise to expression, is to be in that state of the universal consciousness—which is indicated in this body here, Edgar Cayce, through which there is given this interpretation for [2475].

[22]So, in analyzing all this—first study the variations of what has been the body-temperament, in thought, in food. For, the body-physical becomes that which it assimilates from material nature. The body-mental becomes that it assimilates from both the physical-mental and the spiritual-mental. The soul is *all* of that the entity is, has been or may be.

[23]Then, *who* and *what* would the entity have to direct self in such experiences?

[24]To be loosed without a governor, or a director, may easily become harmful.

[25]But as we would give, from here, let not such a director be that of an entity. Rather so surround self with the universal consciousness of the *Christ* as to be directed by that influence as may be committed to thee.

[26]Thus the entity may use constructively that which has been attained.

[27]But to prevent physical harm, mental harm—attune self in body and in mind with that influence by which the entity seeks to be directed; not haphazardly, not by chance, but—as of old—choose thou this day *whom* ye will serve: the living God within thee, by thee, through thee? or those influences of knowledge without wisdom, that would enslave or empower thee with the material things which only gratify for the moment?

[28]Rather choose thou as he of old—let others do as they may, but as for thee, serve thou the living God.

[29]Thus ye may constructively use that ability of spiritual attunement, which is the birthright of each soul; ye may use it as a helpful influence in thy experiences in the earth.

[30]But make haste *slowly!* Prepare the body. Prepare the mind, before ye attempt to loosen it in such measures or manners that it may be taken hold upon by those influences which constantly seek expressions of self rather than of a living, constructive influence of a *crucified* Savior.

[31]Then, crucify desire in self; that ye may be awakened to the real abilities of helpfulness that lie within thy grasp.

[32]Ready for questions.

[33](Q) Is there at present any danger to any particular body-function, such as sex; or to general health?

(A) As we have indicated, without preparation, desires of *every* nature may become so accentuated as to destroy—or to overexercise as to bring detrimental forces; unless the desire and purpose is acknowledged and set *in* the influence of self as to its direction—when loosened by the kundaline activities through the body.

[34](Q) Just what preparation would you advise for the body, now?

(A) This should be rather the choice of the body from its *own* development, than from what *any* other individual entity or source might give.

Purify the body, purify the mind; that the principle, the choice of ideals as made by the entity may be made manifest.

Do whatever is required for this—whether the washing of the body, the surrounding with this or that influence, or that of whatever nature.

As has been experienced, this opening of the centers or the raising of the life force may be brought about by certain characters of breathing—for, as indicated, the breath is power in itself; and this power may be directed to certain portions of the body. But for what purpose? As yet it has been only to see what will happen! Remember what curiosity did to the cat! Remember what curiosity did to Galileo, and what it did to Watt—but they used it in quite different directions in each case!

[35](Q) Considering the development of the entity, is further practice of the yoga exercises of breathing and meditation recommended?

(A) By all means! if and when, and *only* when, preparation has been made; and when there is the knowledge, the understanding and the wisdom as to what to do *with* that gained! Without such, do not undertake same!

[36]We are through for the present.

Chapter 15

THE WORKSHOP OF MARRIAGE

READING 480-20

When I study a Cayce reading, I often create in my mind a modern language adaptation. Personally, I don't think or speak in the same language structures as the readings. Creating for myself a version of the words that's "closer to home" makes it easier for me to do something very important with that reading—namely, to help it come alive in my everyday thinking and in my daily deeds.

I don't find that I need to do this for every reading. Sometimes the poetic quality of a reading is perfect for me just the way it is. But for other readings it's extraordinarily helpful to me if I make an adaptation into more familiar language patterns. I offer the following example as an "interpretation" simply to illustrate what you may want to try for yourself on occasion:

Mrs. Cayce: The soul-entity [480]. Considering her past and present development, together with the opportunities in this present life, you will advise her regarding her adjustment to the new life before her. You will answer the questions that may be asked regarding her coming marriage, as well as information in her previous life reading from this psychic source.

Mr. Cayce: Yes, we have the soul-entity now called

[480] and the information that was given in her previous reading about physical and mental factors, plus the necessary attributes for her to change spiritually—that is, to experience soul development.

In the changes that are just ahead for this soul-entity, it would be very advisable to consider carefully several conditions. Always remember this:

All that can be offered here as counsel or advice is to describe what would be ideal—but without becoming unrealistically idealistic. Some conditions that come into your life are necessary influences and challenges. And in those cases, there is nothing that can be advised except to use your free will and make a choice to apply, to live out, what you hold as an ideal.

As you and your husband-to-be make choices along the way, both of you may find something very important in the new relationship: You have the ability to make the very best conditions and surroundings for each other—ones that will be most helpful for mental and soul development for the two of you.

But all of this depends on the two of you making some adjustments in that direction, that you both take thought of what is needed and necessary in the experience of the other.

As has been indicated earlier, the two of you will find that you are a complement one to another in a great many ways.

Your own natural tendency is to be the leader, the one who provides the impelling influence. Do not let this, then, overshadow the abilities or the activities of the mate in *any* way or manner. This advice does not mean to become subservient to his ideas—in your own thinking or physical behavior. But instead, let both of you give and take, knowing that this is to be a fifty-fifty proposition, with you each supplying that which is best within yourselves.

For example, there will be situations which at the time make one of you feel that the other is being negligent and unfairly requiring too much patient waiting. But the one who is being put upon should not rail and complain at such times or allow such events to become a stumbling block. Instead, always try to *reason* well together.

In those things that have to do with your social life, be considerate of each other. *Know* that it is necessary for both of you to be as interested in the activities of the other as if those activities were a part and parcel and portion of yourself. This does *not* mean to adopt a demanding attitude. You each can live your own life, each having your own interests, each having your own responsibilities; but at the same time, each of you supplying what is necessary in various social activities so that there is harmony and cooperation.

Let both of you budget your time well. Give a certain amount of time to recreation for the body, for the mind, for the social activities, and for any other necessary activity that meets an important need. And be *cooperative* with each other in such things.

And do not forget to include time for recuperative forces in your lives. For example, be sure to include entertainment. These recuperative forces actually make your talents and abilities more effective in all phases of human experience, especially as you work to coordinate your lives with each other.

As we have told you earlier, marriage will be an effective, helpful experience for you—and for your mate—if you coordinate your activities in the relationship. Make your ideas and actions together sacred: not for self-indulgence but instead as a union of whatever it takes for the Creative Forces to be active in both your lives. Marriage can then be like a crowning influence in the lives of you and your husband.

As you establish a home, make it after the pattern of a

heavenly home. It is not to be merely a place set aside to sleep or to rest. Rather, it can be somewhere that you *and* everyone who enters may feel and experience something special by the very vibrations the two of you have created.

These vibrations come from you and your husband holding the home as sacred, as a place of helpfulness. It will create a *hopefulness* in the air all about your home. This kind of home will not only be a place of rest, not only a place of recreation for the mind, not only a haven for the bodies and minds of the two of you, but also for every person that comes as a visitor or guest. And remember that teaching that you have heard in many past lives: Be mindful as you entertain guests, because some people have entertained angels without being aware of it.

Make your home, your abode, a place where an angel would *desire* to visit, where an angel would seek to be a guest. For it will bring greater blessings, greater glories, greater contentment and satisfaction. It is a glorious harmony when you can adjust yourself and your relationship to each other in this way.

Do not say to yourselves, "We'll do it tomorrow—we'll do it next week—we'll make such a home next year." Instead, let what you sow in your relationships day by day be the seeds of truth and hope. As they grow and bear fruit in your relationships—as the days, months, and years go by—they will grow into that garden of beauty that indeed makes for the home. In *every* association with someone—with each other as marriage partners, with friends, with strangers who visit you—let a *hopeful, helpful* spirit direct more and more often your attitudes and actions. And as these relationships grow and mature toward harvest, the *Lord* may give the increase.

If you have mentally created a home environment in which hate, envy, malice, and jealousy are the fruits, then this can bring only dissension, strife, and hardships. But if the seeds of truth and life are sown, then the fruits—as your married life together goes on—will be in harmony. And He, the Father, who is the guide in everything, will bless you, even as He has promised from the beginning. If you will seek just that, through the union of your desires and purposes being focused on what is important spiritually, then the fruits of your bodies may bless many people.

None of this is to say that your lives should become overly serious—long-faced—or that no joy should enter in! *Rather* be *joyous* always in your *living,* in your associations and activities. Joy and happiness produce more joy and happiness—unless the focus is *selfish.*

But when doubts, fears, and troubles arise (as surely they will because they do in everyone's experience), come together before the throne of grace and mercy, as you can find in meditation before the Lord. Take your troubles to God, not to other people! For He is merciful, whereas other people may be unkind, jealous, hard-hearted, set, and determined. When you face a challenging decision, take it to God. Then make your decision so that whether it is yes or no, that choice comes from God.

All of this advice will require that you make some adjustments in your ways and manners of living. But as you do so, you will bring into your experience the greater glory of the Father in the earth.

Ready for questions.

(Q) In what former incarnation did I know my husband-to-be?

(A) This is not the time for that information to be given. It can come when the time is right.

(Q) What is our greatest purpose together in this life?

(A) Harmony!

(Q) How may I express and live up to the highest ideals in marriage?

(A) It has been indicated already in this reading.

(Q) As my life reading stated that I might attain to the best in this experience through music or drama, how may I coordinate this with marriage and still express the highest in both?

(A) What kind of music is potentially in an earthly home? As stated earlier, a physical home can be an emblem of the heavenly home. As you work toward trying to harmonize career and home, you'll attune yourself to the music of the spheres—to a heavenly music. This is what can be contacted in the highest human achievement in the earth: the *home!*

We are through for the present time.

THE READING

This psychic reading, 480-20, was given by Edgar Cayce on July 22, 1935. The conductor was Gertrude Cayce.

[1]GC: Entity, [480]. Considering her past and present development, together with opportunities in this present life, you will advise her regarding her adjustment to the new life before her. You will answer the questions that may be asked regarding her coming marriage and information given in her life reading through these sources.

[2]EC: Yes, we have the entity known as or called in the present [480], and the information that has been given through these channels respecting the physical, the mental and the attributes necessary for change in the spiritual or soul development.

[3]In the approach, then, to those changes that are eminent in the mind of this entity in the present, well that all these conditions be taken into consideration; remembering ever as this:

[4]Only counsel may be given, only those conditions that are as ideal without being idealistic, those condi-

tions that are as necessary influences without there being other than the choice of the entity in making for the
application of same in the experience.

[5]For as the ways are chosen before thee, you each may
find in the new associations and relations the ability to
make the best conditions, the surroundings, the experiences that will bring into the experience of each that
which will be the most helpful in the soul and development mentally of each; provided the adjustments are
made in those directions, with the thought of that necessary in the experience of each to make for such.

[6]As indicated, these will find that they are a complement one to another in a great many ways.

[7]The natural tendency of the entity, [480], is to be the
leader, the impelling influence. Do not let this, then,
overshadow the abilities or the activities of the mate in
any way or manner. This does not mean to become, from
the mental or the material side, as subservient to his
ideas; but let each give and take, knowing that this is to
be a fifty-fifty proposition, with you each supplying that
which is best within yourselves.

[8]When the necessities are such as to require waiting
and patience even, in those things that may at the time
appear to be as negligence on the part of the one or the
other, do not rail at such times or allow those things to
become stumbling blocks; but always *reason* well together.

[9]In those things that pertain to the social life, be considerate one of the other. *Know* that there is the necessity of you each being as interested in the activities of
the other as though they were a part and parcel and portion of yourselves. Not in a *demanding* attitude, but you
each living your own life, each having your own interests, each having your own responsibilities; and each
supplying those necessary influences or forces in each
association as to make for a harmonious cooperative

activity in such social activities as may be had in every phase of the experience.

[10]Let each budget the time. Let each give so much to the recreation for the body, for the mind, for the social activities, for the necessary activities for the supplying of the needs in their varied relationships. And be *cooperative* one with another in such things.

[11]Let also there be time for the recuperative forces necessary in the experience, those that may be added as elements in the entertainment, the necessary forces for the adding to the *effects* of the abilities in all phases of human experience as correlated to the coordinating of the lives one with another.

[12]The marital relationships, as we have indicated, will become an effectual, helpful experience in the life of the entity; as also in the life of the mate, if the coordinations of their activities in such relationships are made as to be sacred in their notions, their ideas, their activities being not for self-indulgences but as a union of that necessary for the creative forces and influences in the experiences of the life of each, as to bring the crowning influence to the experience of each.

[13]In the establishing of the home, make it as that which may be the pattern of a heavenly home. Not as that set aside for only a place to sleep or to rest, but where not only self but all who enter there may feel, may experience, by the very vibrations that are set up by each in the sacredness of the home, a helpfulness, a *hopefulness* in the air *about* the home. As not only a place of rest, not only a place of recreation for the mind, not only a place as a haven for the bodies and minds of both but for all that may be as visitors or as guests. And remember those injunctions that have been in thine experience in many of thine sojourns, and be thou mindful of the entertaining of the guests; for some have entertained angels unawares. Make thine home, thine abode, where an angel

would *desire* to visit, where an angel would seek to be a guest. For it will bring the greater blessings, the greater glories, the greater contentment, the greater satisfaction; the glorious harmony of adjusting thyself and thy relationships one with another in making same ever harmonious. Do not begin with, "We will do it tomorrow—we will begin next week—we will make for such next year." Let that thou sowest in thy relationships day by day be the seeds of truth, of hope, that as they grow to fruition in thy relationships, as the days and the months and the years that are to come go by, they will grow into that garden of beauty that makes indeed for the home.

[14]In *every* association, whether one with another in thy relationships or with thy own friends, or with the strangers that enter, let thy activities be such that there may come more and more of that which is *directed* by the spirit of *hopefulness, helpfulness,* in thy attitudes one to another.

[15]And as these grow to the harvest in life, the *Lord* may give the increase.

[16]If ye have builded such that hate, envy, malice, jealousy are the fruits of same, these can only bring dissension and strife and hardships. But if the seeds of truth and life are sown, then the fruition—as the life goes on together—will be in harmony. And He, the Father, being thy guide in all will bless thee, even as He has promised from the beginning. For in the fruit of thy bodies may many be blessed, if ye will but seek that *through* the union of thy purposes, of thy desires, with their import in things spiritual, such may come to pass.

[17]Not that the life is to be made long-faced, that no joy is to enter in! *Rather* be ye *joyous* in thy *living,* in thine association, in thy activities, ever. For joy and happiness *beget* joy and happiness; unless the import be of a *selfish* nature.

[18]But when doubts and fears and troubles arise (as

they must, as they will in the experience of all), come ye rather together before the throne of grace and mercy, as may be found in the meditation before the Lord. Take thine troubles to Him, not to thy fellow man! For *He* is merciful when *man* may be unkind, jealous, hard-hearted, set, determined. But let thy yeas be yea in the Lord; let thy nays be nay in the Lord.

[19]And in adjusting thyself in these ways and manners ye may bring to thine experience the greater glory of the Father in the earth.

[20]Ready for questions.

[21](Q) In what former incarnation did I know [633]?

(A) These will be given in their proper order.

[22](Q) What is our greatest purpose together in this life?

(A) Harmony!

[23](Q) How may I express and live up to the highest ideals in marriage?

(A) As has been indicated.

[24](Q) As my life reading [480-1] gave that I might attain to the best in this experience through music or the play, how may I coordinate same with marriage and express the highest in both?

(A) For in the home is the music of what? As indicated, it is an emblem of the heavenly home. And as these are made into the harmonious experiences that may come in the associations, they may bring indeed the music of the spheres in the activities as one with another, and those that must be contacted in the highest of man's achievement in the earth—the *home!*

[25]We are through for the present.

Chapter 16

STAYING CONNECTED TO THE FUNDAMENTALS

READING 262-1

Several years ago I unexpectedly encountered a man with whom I'd been acquainted for a number of years through our mutual involvement in the A.R.E. When our paths crossed one morning in the A.R.E. headquarters library, we exchanged greetings, and he said, "I'm rather surprised you're still working here. I'd have thought that by now you'd have outgrown the Cayce material." His statement stopped me short.

I can no longer recall exactly how I answered him. I suspect I said something about the rich diversity of the Cayce readings that still held my interest. Even if I'm now vague about the details of my response, what *did* stick with me—in my long-term memory—was his *question.* I guess I hadn't seriously considered the idea that the Cayce readings' philosophy was something you outgrow and then move beyond, to more advanced spiritual studies. I *still* find myself wondering, "Do many people think that way?"

But there is a question far more significant than my longevity as a staff member.

"Why should we so intently study inspired, clairvoyantly derived information that was produced sixty or seventy years ago? Aren't there smarter alternatives that we could choose? For example, why shouldn't A.R.E. keep careful, archival records of Cayce's work, but turn our primary focus to contemporary psychic sources and spiritual philosophies?"

This is a tough question. Organizationally, we're very interested in contemporary findings, and one need look only at our book and conference catalogs to see the indisputable evidence. Nonetheless, the Cayce readings remain our central interest, and I believe the reason is far more profound than tradition or old habits.

Consider this idea: There is something very special about an activity or enterprise at its inception. A clear impulse often comes through. Admittedly, there can be a certain innocence about some of the deeper issues and challenges that lie ahead. But in that foundation impulse there is a kind of pure vision which—even missing certain complexities yet to come—nevertheless needs always to be honored and kept very special. One has only to look at human love relations to see the principle at work on a small scale—the bond between a parent and newborn child, or the sometimes naive love that can first bring marriage partners together.

I suggest that the Cayce readings themselves were a primary impulse in a cultural movement that has now begun to flower as holistic medicine, transpersonal psychology, and a more ecumenical vision of world religions. The readings contain wisdom and pure vision of renewed spirituality—something that is timeless. Certainly there are contemporary spiritual teachers and consciousness researchers who go into topics that Cayce never addressed, into subjects he never mentioned. And there is much to gain from their serious study. But just as surely, there is something irreplaceable about the initiating impulse of a movement. We can never go wrong—as far as I can see—going back to basics and rediscovering the spiritual soundness and clear perspective of what Cayce presented sixty and seventy years ago.

What could be more basic to the Cayce philosophy than the first reading in the *A Search for God* lesson sequence? This reading on cooperation is an excellent starting point for any inquirer about Cayce, as well as being a wonderful set of principles for any experienced student who needs to reconnect with the fundamentals.

This opening discourse on cooperation demonstrates my point. Vital themes are highlighted. In paragraph 4, Cayce emphasizes the importance of finding one's own special calling to serve. Then he reminds us of a central biblical promise: We can do even greater things than Jesus simply because the Christ Consciousness lives in every human soul, and it's available to express creatively.

What comes through, too, is the social dimension of Cayce's philosophy (see paragraph 7, especially). It's lesson number one: doing things cooperatively with each other through a commonality of purpose and ideal (even if sometimes there are differences of opinion or idea).

And finally, this "back to basics" reading underscores the inescapable moral message that is at the heart of the Cayce view of soul growth—that is, service. " . . . holy is he that seeks to be a light to his brother . . . Bear ye one another's burdens . . . "

In retrospect, maybe I should have pulled this reading from the shelves and shown it to my friend when he admitted surprise that I hadn't yet grown beyond Cayce. I would have been forced to admit that I'm still working on these fundamentals!

THE READING

This psychic reading, 262-1, was given by Edgar Cayce on September 14, 1931. The conductor was Gertrude Cayce.

¹GC: You will have before you the group gathered in this room, who desire—as a group—to be guided through these forces as to how they may best be a channel in presenting to the world the truth and light needed. You will answer the questions which this group will ask.

²EC: Yes, we have the group—as a group—as gathered here, seeking to be a channel that they, as a group, as individuals, may be—and give—the light to the waiting world.

³As each have gathered here—as each gathered here has been associated in their various experiences in the earth, as each has prepared themselves for a channel through these experiences—so may they, as a group, combine their efforts in a cooperative manner to give to the individual, the group, the classes, the masses, that as they receive, as they have gained in this experience.

⁴To some are given to be teachers, to some are given to be healers, to some are given to be interpreters. Let each, then, do *their* job and their part *well, in* the manner as is given *to* them, knowing—in the forces as manifest through them—they become, then, a light in *their* own respective action and field of endeavor. As the forces manifest in their various ways and manners, to some will be given those of prophecy, to some will be given those of teaching, to some will be given those of ministration, to some as ministers. Then, in the ways as they present themselves; for, as has been given, he that receives shall give, he that cometh together in that name that will give, even as has been promised, "as I have given and am *in* the Father, so in *Me* may *ye* do as I have done, and *greater* things than I have done shall ye do, for I go *to* the Father, and ye in me, as ye ask in my name, so shall it be *done* unto you!"

⁵Then, as there cometh in the minds, hearts, souls of each, so will there be given—in that selfsame hour—*that* as *ye* shall do!

[6]Ready for questions.

[7](Q) Outline for us the steps which we must take that we may become more of one mind, that we may be of the greatest influence for good.

(A) As should be for each to learn that first *lesson* as should be given unto others: Let all dwell together in mind as of one purpose, one aim; or, *first* learn coopera- tion! Learn what that means in a *waiting*, in a *watchful*, in a world *seeking to* know, *to* see, a sign. There, as has been given, will only *be* the sign *given to* those that have drunk of the cup that *makes* for cooperation in *every sense* of enlightening a seeking desiring world. Cast not pearls before swine, neither be thou overanxious for the moment. *Wait* ye on the Lord; for, as has been promised, he that *seeks* shall find, and ye *will* receive—each of you—powers from on high. *Use* that in a constructive, in a manner as befits that desire of the group, of each. Think not of thine *own* desire, but let that mind be in you as was in Him, as may be in all those *seeking* the way.

[8](Q) If it be acceptable to the [higher or universal] forces, direct us as to how we may best prepare a course of lessons for this and similar groups.

(A) First let each prepare themselves and receive that as will be given unto each in *their respective* sphere of development, of desire, of ability. The first *lesson*—as has been given—learn what it means to cooperate in *one* mind, in *God's* way; for, as each would prepare them- selves, in meditating day and night, in "What wilt thou have *me* do, O Lord?" and the *answer will* be *definite*, clear, to each as are gathered here, will they seek in His name; for He is *among* you in this present hour, for all as *seek* are in that attitude of prayer. Pray *ye*, that ye may be *acceptable* to Him in thy going ins and coming outs; for holy is he that seeks to be a light to his brother; and faints not in the trials nor the temptations, for He tempts *none* beyond that they are *able* to bear. Bear ye one another's burdens, in that each fills his *own* heart—as is *given, answer* when He calls—"Here am I, send me."

[9](Q) What would be the best subject for the first lesson?

(A) Cooperation. Let each seek for that as will be *their* part in this lesson, and *it* will be given each as *they* ask for same.

[10]We are through for the present.

You Can Receive Books Like This One and Much, Much More

You can begin to receive books in the *A.R.E. Membership Series* and many more benefits by joining the nonprofit Association for Research and Enlightenment, Inc., as a Sponsoring or Life member.

The A.R.E. has a worldwide membership that receives a wide variety of study aids, all aimed at assisting individuals in their spiritual, mental, and physical growth.

Every member of A.R.E. receives a copy of *Venture Inward*, the organization's bimonthly magazine; an in-depth journal, *The New Millennium*, on alternate months; opportunity to borrow, through the mail, from a collection of more than 500 files on medical and metaphysical subjects; access to one of the world's most complete libraries on metaphysical and spiritual subjects; and opportunities to participate in conferences, international tours, a retreat-camp for children and adults, and numerous nationwide volunteer activities.

In addition to the foregoing benefits, Sponsoring and Life members also receive as gifts three books each year in the *A.R.E. Membership Series*.

If you are interested in finding out more about membership in A.R.E. and the many benefits that can assist you on your path to fulfillment, you can easily contact the Membership Department by writing Membership, A.R.E., P.O. Box 595, Virginia Beach, VA 23451-0595 or by calling **1-800-333-4499** or faxing **1-757-422-6921**.

**Explore our electronic visitor's center on the Internet:
http://www.are-cayce.com**